DESIGNED FOR DEPENDENCY

LORI A. VARICK, M.ED.

Emerald Books

P.O. Box 635
Lynnwood, Washington 98046

DESIGNED FOR DEPENDENCY

Published by Emerald Books
Lynnwood, Washington 98046

ISBN 1-883002-04-4

94 95 96 97 98 99 00 – 10 9 8 7 6 5 4 3 2 1

*This book is lovingly dedicated to my
Abba Father for the gift of dependency;
to my colleague and best friend, Linda Walsh;
and to Warren, Anna, and Kirsten.*

Acknowledgments

I am now convinced that the writing of a book does not occur without the assistance of many willing helpers. In my case, it's been the support and patience of my clients, friends, and colleagues that have made this possible. I would like to express my special gratitude to:

Linda Walsh, who has taught me a great deal about emotional vulnerability and who helped me work on the manuscript.

Warren Walsh, my friend, publisher, and cheerleader in the faith.

Anna and Kirsten, for their patience while I have been writing. We will play again!

Angela Sauer, for her editorial assistance. I couldn't have done this without her.

Carol and Gretchen, Jennine and Katie, for bailing me out over and over again.

My pastors, Bill Robinson and Joe Schneider, for their support and encouragement both in my counseling practice and in the writing of this book. Their godliness has greatly impacted my life personally and my theological understanding.

Ron Boehme, my father in the faith and friend in the warfare.

Colleen, who provided chicken soup and kindness when I was writing.

My mom and dad, who have taught me never to give up.

Contents

Preface

Part One: Beginning The Journey

Introduction

Part Two: Understanding The Journey

Part Three: Completing the Journey

Epilogue

Preface

There is some confusion about the terms *dependent, interdependent,* and *independent.* Since other books have been written in depth about these concepts, I will not provide a lengthy discourse here. It is important, however, to understand these terms as they relate to the Lord and to us as His children.

Dependence

People who are dependent need to have others provide things for them that they cannot provide for themselves. Such is the case with babies and children, the sick, and often the very old. Such is also the case for Christians who recognize the depth of their need for Christ. Dependency on God means that we acknowledge His right and responsibility to lead us, to provide for our needs, and to someday take us home. Our deepest needs and longings are in His hand; His plans are in our hearts.

Whether we wish to acknowledge it or not, we are dependent on God for everything. God is the Creator and Sustainer of all life. The vigor that comes with accepting this blissful state of weakness is priceless. We can rest in His love and absolute goodness, in the knowledge that we belong, in the unfathomable richness of His kind heart, and in the assurance of His justice. In its truest sense, dependency on God allows us to accept and respond to His role as our Heavenly Father in our most intimate relationship.

Independence

Being independent means that a person doesn't feel the need to open his/her heart, soul, mind, and strength to anyone. God is someone to call upon in time of need, but not as a daily companion, guide, or authority in the life of an independent person. Independence is often an illusion for those who fear vulnerability and struggle with emotional detachment. Others are allowed to come close enough to be useful but are stopped short of passing through the gate of self-disclosure. Independence is not an admirable state, for dwelling within it are loneliness and isolation.

Interdependence

Interdependence is found in healthy relationships of all kinds; it is the perfect dance between dependency and independence. Those who are interdependent acknowledge the emotional need of intimacy and enjoy its mutual benefits.

Interdependence as it relates to human relationships recognizes a healthy need for others but knows when to let go. This concept has inherent qualities that are attractive to humans relating to each other, but must not be found in their relationship with God. While we are desperately needy of Him, the opposite is not true. Although God cares deeply about us, with all our dusty emotions and flaws, He does not need us.

PART ONE

Beginning
the Journey

"Then I said to you, 'Don't be frightened.
Don't be afraid of those people.
The Lord your God will go ahead of you.
He will fight for you as He did in Egypt.
You saw Him do it.
In the desert you saw how
the Lord your God carried you.
He was like a man carrying his son.
He has brought you safely all the way to this place.'
But you still did not trust the Lord your God.
As you moved, He went before you.
He found places for you to camp.
He went before you in a fire at night
and in a cloud during the day.
He showed you which way to go."

Deuteronomy 1:29–32

Introduction

Lord God, you are my hope.
I have trusted you since I was young.
I have depended on you since I was born.
You have been my help from the day I was born.
I will always praise you.

Psalm 71:5–6

*D*esigned For Dependency is intended to spark a fire of passion that will encourage you to honestly engage the Lord in battle. Ask yourself questions about God's design: Has He created us to be dependent on Him? Why is it so hard? Why at times does He seem so distant and aloof?

Dependency as it is often used today implies an insatiable neediness that strikes at the heart of all we value. To need is to lack; to lack is to be weak; to be weak is to be despised. Those who flounder in the pool of swirling neediness often feel the anxious gasp that comes just prior to drowning. The sheer need of needing produces a level of self-contempt that can seldom be uttered.

People tend to believe all that is loved, all that is valued, belongs to those fortunate enough to be independent. This, of course is a myth, for no one is truly free from need. We derive our life from the flow of oxygen, the sustenance of food, the quenching refreshment of water, and, yes, the inexplicit nurturance of life that comes from being human and relating.

To acknowledge weakness and dependency is to acknowledge humanity. To be human is to need. If all we possess is images of futility, then to see life in its reality is to find hopelessness, tragedy, and despair. To engage life is to do battle...and often lose.

If we are independent, we need only those things that are impersonal, for we have learned to despise dependency. We are free to seek our own value in impersonal things. Lost in illusion and fantasy, we may relate independently to those who share our contempt for life and weakness. We may speak boldly with assertiveness and strength, daring those more dependent to challenge our walls of isolation.

Many of us have built walls to protect ourselves, but the piercing reality of our shame causes us to tremble with fear. We are torn, and we are dependent. We have believed that we are not and should not be dependent, for to depend on someone else implies an existing trust. (If I am to be dependent on you for my deepest needs, you can't fail me, or I will die. But alas, you did fail me, and I have died.) We want that which others cannot offer and crave things only heaven can provide. We will choose someone or something to feed our longings and insatiable desires, which do not go away, for God made them to live.

Living death is the absence of someone good to meet my needs. We have been designed by God to be dependent on Him. King David's belief was that God's presence and help could be counted on from the day of his birth (Psalm 71:6).

We must depend on God to teach us to love dependency and to despise our own futile efforts to strive to be independent of Him. God is immensely powerful and never tires of our intensity. He is able to endure our pleading prayers and concerns and to listen patiently to the foolish ramblings of His inquisitive children. He becomes to us a sweet, unpredictable, and yet irresistible Love who invites us to come to His table. We may shake with fear at the thought of offending Him, for we know what He can do to an enemy; yet we may race to Him when we have failed, confident that He will compassionately soothe our fragile hearts.

Choosing to be dependent requires that we yield our own direction and control. It necessitates a trust in a God who is very good to those who love Him but Who turns His face from those who become His enemy. Do you secretly fear that you are His enemy?

I pray that reading *Designed for Dependency* will help you understand why you hide from relational intimacy and show you how to heal from past wounds. Engage God in a battle to the death—your death—and experience a rejuvenating awakening that will "stun you into silence."

Chapter 1

The Search
For Understanding

My child, believe what I say.
And remember what I command you.
Listen to wisdom.
Try with all your heart to gain understanding.
Cry out for wisdom. Beg for understanding.
Search for it as you would for silver.
Hunt for it like hidden treasure.
Then you will understand
what it means to respect the Lord.
Then you will begin to know God.

Proverbs 2:1–5

*N*umerous insightful and scholarly Christian books are available today to victims of abuse, largely because people have been forced to deal with the reality of childhood trauma and its impact on them as adults. Our own understanding of the clinical and spiritual aspects of helping others has been greatly enhanced by the growing number of Christian counselors who are using Scripture as their primary resource for healing.

❦   ❦   ❦   ❦   ❦

In the recovery movement, both Christian and secular, we have been taught to focus on ourselves—our needs, losses, traumas, and rights.

❦   ❦   ❦   ❦   ❦

For years, a steady array of self–actualization books have been encouraging us to take control of our lives and to start over again. We no longer have to be victims; we are survivors. Refusing to be pushed around or held down any longer, we are confronting our parents, spouses, children—anyone who has ever hurt us.

The pendulum has swung from one extreme to the other. At first we were given a license to express ourselves and our anger—which we did—wounding and inflicting damage to those who, in many cases, were not aware that they had hurt us so deeply. This is true with many parents who were raised in an era when loving their children meant putting a roof over their heads, food on the table, and clothes on their backs. Many parents and grandparents who lived through the Depression were poverty stricken and knew literally what it was to go without; it took everything simply to survive. To be confronted in their sixties and seventies for failing to provide nurturing, self–esteem, bonding, attachment, etc., could not be understood. As a result, rather than experiencing healing and restoration, many of us faced deeper wounds and isolation in our effort to honestly communicate to those who had hurt us about our pain.

Sensing that the recovery community has somehow gotten off track, professional prophets are now telling us that it's no good to focus on ourselves. We need to focus outward and upward to heal. (This too is an old message.) Many of us have become exhausted truth seekers who have every conceivable recovery brand name etched on our psyches and on our souls. In human terms, we are confused! To lessen our confusion, we need to understand the following:

1) God's standard for the provision of basic security needs in the areas of physical, emotional, spiritual, and intellectual development. (In other words, what do we need to grow up healthy?)
2) Who is supposed to provide these needs.
3) What happens if, through neglect or abuse, these needs have not been provided.
4) How we heal if our basic needs have not been met. (Are we doomed to be dysfunctional forever because we didn't get something we needed as a child?)
5) God's response and solution to all these questions.

Since most of us retain only a fraction of what we read or process, we need a tool to use in therapy that will both address these questions and be comprehensive, thorough, and uncompromised insofar as Scripture is concerned. Ultimately, we need a resource that will help us understand why we struggle as adults, one that will be useful as a biblical standard in our own healing process as well as one to use while training our own children.

The fact is that most parents, including Christians, replay what they learned, even in those areas that were personally hurtful. To break well–defined generational habits, we need to understand not only biblical solutions but also how experiences from our early development impact the rest of our lives. The enthusiasm and fruit of God's solutions teach us that healing is not the end, but rather a means to restoration with the Lord, ourselves, and others.

Because of God's great kindness and tender love, we can experience a level of emotional healing that will allow us to honestly know and love Him in the depths of our hearts. We do not have to be victims or survivors; rather we can be servants and children of our glorious God. The end result of our healing will never be self–actualization. Rather, we will have the privilege of learning to love our Lord with "wholehearted devotion and a willing mind" (I Chronicles 28:9). Instead of focusing inward to find strength, we will cry out to Jesus for help in our time of need and embrace our weakness (Hebrews 4:14–16). Our relationships will improve, not only because of new boundaries we set but also as a result of obedience to biblical truth, an obedience that flows out of earnest love and relationship with the Lord.

The truth is, God's solution to our brokenness (as laid out for us in Scripture) will never head the list of recovery resources, simply because the message is a difficult one. To heal, we have to trust Him. To trust, we have to deal with the reasons we don't trust anyone and be willing to yield control.

To stop controlling, we have to become willing to let someone else dictate our destiny, someone we may believe failed us when we needed Him most. To heal means we lower our walls of self–protection and allow Jesus to restore us in His own way. To do that, we must see Him as someone who is safe. Most people who were injured emotionally as children believe that no one is safe or trustworthy. Consequently, victims of childhood abuse or neglect seldom let the One they need most into their fragile hearts.

One of the purposes of *Designed for Dependency* is to help wounded people understand why they suffer, why they don't trust, and why it is essential that they learn to trust in order to heal. Contrary to the recovery messages that flaunt independence or even interdependence as the goal, in reality, we must grow to become utterly dependent on our Abba Father. It has never been His desire for us to move one inch from His heart, nor will it ever be. Relational appropriateness is readily understood when we finally reach that place where there is no God but God in our hearts (Jeremiah 2:5,11–13).

Unfortunately, many of us are still worldly, looking for quick fixes and new drugs of choice to soothe our damaged souls. Not finding what we want, we try to get our insatiable needs fulfilled through others. The list of unfulfilled expectations becomes lengthy, with each loss hardening the wall of self–protection and deepening our numbness.

As you read *Designed for Dependency*, you will be able to specifically evaluate areas of wounding from your past.

Those doubting Thomases who have a hard time believing that God can get the job done in their heart might recall that the original Thomas went on to be a powerful man of God in India and impacted thousands of lives through the power of Christ's resurrection!

Common problems that result from specific unmet needs require Biblical solutions. As we go through each critical area and examine the core beliefs you have developed, remember to thank the Lord for healthy provisions received in childhood and for your parents or caregivers who supplied them. Try to be open to what the Lord would like to show you about the pain you experienced and His solutions for healing wounds that are still raw.

Ultimately, the losses and gains of this world will pale as we anticipate the eternity waiting for us. As Paul noted in his letter to the Christians at Philippi:

At one time all these things were important to me.

But now I think those things are worth nothing because

of Christ. Not only those things, but I think

> *that all things are worth nothing compared with the*
> *greatness of knowing Christ Jesus my Lord.*
> *Because of Christ, I have lost all those things.*
> *And now I know that all those things are worthless trash.*
> *This allows me to have Christ and to belong to him...*

Philippians 3:7–9

As we await that glorious day, there is much to be done. Your pain and brokenness, as horrible as they may feel, should never keep you from serving the Lord or others in His name. Whether you are new to the recovery journey or a weary veteran, these pages should encourage you toward greater dependency on God and fulfilling relationships in the years to come. The wonderful benefit is that you will experience emotional healing as you walk with Him through each step of His divine restoration process.

Chapter 2

Wounding The Hearts of Children

At that time the disciples came to Jesus and asked,
"Who's the greatest in the kingdom of heaven?"
He called a little child and had him stand among them.
And he said: "I tell you the truth, unless you change
and become like little children, you will never enter
the kingdom of heaven....
But, if anyone causes one of these little ones
who believe in me to sin, it would be better for him
to have a large millstone hung around his neck
and to be drowned in the depths of the sea.
Woe to the world because of the things
that cause people to sin! Such things must come,
but woe to the man through whom they come!"

Matthew 18:1-3,6,7

*D*uring recent years, it has become evident that the single greatest cause of problems faced in adulthood can be traced back to family of origin. Painful events of the past have left deep wounds and festering emotional sores. In most cases, the result of childhood trauma is evident in unhappy marriages, family breakups, and strained relationships.

A counselor can help people understand the roots of their problems and work with them on a gradual plan of healing and restoration. Searching for the roots inevitably leads back through a maze of denial, pain, anger, and sadness. The raw emotions of rage become clear as each layer of abuse is removed. Often, middle–aged men and women will weep as they recount incidents of physical, sexual, and emotional abuse when they were small children. We must gently expose the darkness of the violations without exposing the wounded heart of the victim to additional pain.

This darkness has two facets: an external element that can be seen and operates in the physical realm and, less obvious but clearly more dangerous, the darkness that occurs in the spiritual realm of creation. The apostle Paul described it this way: "The devil who rules this world has blinded the minds of those who do not believe....God once said, 'Let the light shine out of the darkness!' And this is the same God who made His light shine in our hearts. He gave us light by letting us know the glory of God that is in the face of Christ" (II Corinthians 4:4,6).

The warfare is between the forces of light (God) and the forces of darkness (Satan). Many readily acknowledge that evil events go on daily, but they fail to understand the spiritual implications. This chapter examines both the physical and spiritual aspects of abuse to present a broader picture of the eternal dynamics involved.

Physical Warfare

Statistically, the harsh realities of familial abuse are staggering, and the true picture is yet unknown. In their book, *Healing Victims of Sexual Abuse*, Heitritter and Vought indicate that a child is sexually abused every two minutes! They further state that less than two percent of molestations are ever reported.

❧   ❧   ❧   ❧   ❧

A major obstacle to recovery is getting past a legalistic, religious theology that forbids people to work through the wounds of the past honestly and instead commands an instantaneous choice for forgiveness.

❧   ❧   ❧   ❧   ❧

Dr. Dan Allender, author of *The Wounded Heart*, cites a recent study in which 38 percent of the women interviewed stated that they had been sexually abused by an adult or family member before the age of 18. These numbers cannot possibly paint a realistic picture of the true damage. Many abuse victims bury the horrid memories from the past, not having the emotional maturity or strength to cope with the trauma. Others fail to connect childhood abuse with adult struggles, minimizing the impact of things that happened years ago.

There is no way to calculate, in addition to the wounding caused by sexual abuse, the damage done to children in the areas of emotional and physical abuse. One of the most horrifying truths being uncovered in the Christian counseling arena is that the incidence of abuse within Christian households is often more prevalent than in unbelieving homes!

A major obstacle to recovery is getting past a legalistic, religious theology that forbids people to work through the wounds of the past honestly and instead commands an instantaneous choice for forgiveness. In *The Wounded Heart*, Dan Allender says, "Forgiveness built on 'forgetfulness' is the Christian version of a frontal lobotomy." True healing requires that we look at our pain honestly, commit to a forgiveness process, and then pray for the courage and commitment to do the hard thing—change.

Unfortunately, the Christian community often fails to identify roots, largely because of a theology that considers digging up the past akin to treading on sacred ground. This is amid the cries of the loud, though not necessarily the correct, that it is sinful to not forgive and forget. In our usual extreme and oftentimes "spiritualized" message, we offer more compassion to the abuser than to the victim.

The creed "We have encountered the enemy and the enemy is us" can be aptly applied to many Christians as they neglect the truth of Scripture in favor of the more pleasant—if not compromised—exhortation to simply forgive and trust Jesus. In reality, Jesus said, "If you hold to my teaching, you are really my disciples. Then you will know the truth, and the truth will set you free" (John 8:31–32). Many of us are not free, because we are afraid of the truth or we refuse to obey Scripture when it comes to more difficult concepts such as "speaking the truth in love" and confronting those who have wounded us (Ephesians 4 and Matthew 18).

The tragedy is that rather than put blame where it belongs, we rage in our hearts toward the Lord, believing that He neither cares about our pain nor has any desire to heal us. After all, we have tried to pray the pain away, faith it away, stuff it away—and still we suffer, angry and disillusioned.

Scripture says, "A man's own folly ruins his life, yet his heart rages against the Lord" (Proverbs 19:3). Sometimes it is the folly of people we should have been able to trust that destroys our tender hearts. Sometimes it is the careless, uncompassionate judgments of other believers that hinder our healing process.

Spiritual Warfare

Apart from the external friction generated between distorted theology and the wounded, there is a more insidious factor that may explain why we are producing yet another generation of emotionally detached young people.

Throughout history, there have been examples of Satan's attempts to destroy babies and small children. We know that there was a demonic scheme to kill Moses and, of course, Jesus many years later. Satan, working behind the scenes with his showcase of demonic weapons, not only would attempt to destroy the man chosen to deliver the Israelites but also, more importantly, would foolishly try to silence the Savior of the world.

Closing our Bibles and opening our eyes to the spiritual warfare that exists today, we can see that Satan has continued to strike at the heart of God by murdering children in record numbers. Innocent and helpless unborn babies are being violently aborted every day. Even as we plead for the lives of the unborn and cry out on their behalf, the evil one has launched yet another sinister plot in which the hearts of children are being destroyed. This is his plot: Scripture tells us that Satan's temporary kingdom is of the world (John 12:31; II Corinthians 4:4). His warfare is ultimately against God (Isaiah 14:13–14); it involves humanity (John 13:27), but it is played out in the spiritual realm (Ephesians 6:12–13).

Satan comes disguised as an angel of light (II Corinthians 11:14), in false benevolence, perverting God's standards. He attacks our hearts, often through human instruments, "roaring like a lion" (I Peter 5:8), to create anxiety, doubt, fear, and panic. He pricks us with thorns (II Corinthians 12:7), ongoing frustrations, and nagging problems to discourage us. He is able to influence and use those not submitted to the Lord by perverting their thinking and behavior (Matthew 15:18–19; John 8:42–45; Romans 1:28). Satan attempts to blind us to the Truth (II Corinthians 4:4; 11:3), tempting us with false enticements and stirring up unsettled memories and feelings from the past (Ephesians 4:26–27).

Satan's desire is to wound God's children in any way

possible. Satan attacks through words (James 3:6–10), creating careless accusations (Revelation 12:2), lashing out at those we love—blaming (Jude 16), criticizing (Acts 11:2), and slandering (Ephesians 4:31). Through gossip (Romans 1:28–32), deception (II Corinthians 4:2), and criticism (Galatians 5:15), hearts are pierced and relationships severed. With fertile territory in the minds and hearts of willing accomplices to evil, Satan appeals to a prideful human nature that aspires to be "like God," which in essence is the desire to be independent of the Lord and in control of our own destinies (Isaiah 14:11–14).

Recognizing that intimacy with God requires willing submission and heartfelt obedience (Philippians 2:8; Isaiah 66:2), Satan purposely attacks the souls of the young, attempting to pervert their understanding of God, His character, and His ways (Matthew 18:6–7; Psalm 10:4–5). Satan seeks to separate us from the Lord through many devices (Ecclesiastes 7:29). In Scripture and in life, numerous "stumbling blocks" impede our spiritual growth and maturation. They can include idols (addictions) (Isaiah 41:29), illusions (incorrect thinking), unresolved bitterness from the past, wrong priorities (people, work, play), or the use of anything that turns our hearts away from rather than toward biblical truth (Jeremiah 5:1–7).

Tired of the "fake it till you make it" disguise, defeated believers numbly replay a lifetime of emptiness and despair. They cannot understand why, after years of sound biblical teaching, they still are unable to feel anything for the Lord and feel very little for anyone else. Life's difficulties and pressures quickly erode their ability to control their anger or their words.

We need to look for the roots of dysfunction, not merely the symptoms that have troubled us. Far below the surface, hidden behind erected walls of self–protection, lies the truth. At first we may struggle to believe that childhood difficulties could have such an impact on adult thinking and behavior. Doesn't time heal? Shouldn't we be able to put things into perspective and go on? Why can't we forgive and forget, as we were taught? Why are we still embittered and distant after so many years?

As adults, we often fail to comprehend the warning signs because we tend to focus blindly on what we can see in the natural realm rather than on the dangers lurking in the spiritual realm. Yet, as believers, we are warned that "our struggle is not against flesh and blood, but against the rulers, against the authorities, against the powers of this dark world, and against the spiritual forces of evil in the heavenly realms" (Ephesians 6:12).

Children lack the knowledge, maturity, and internal strength to stand alone against evil. They are dependent on their caretakers to protect them from the warfare and to shelter them from the storms of life until they have matured. When Satan is able to influence parents to disregard the way of life that God has ordained and, through generation after generation, perverts their beliefs about the Lord, the foundation is laid for self–centered abuse and aggression toward children. Scripture says their consciences become seared and "they have no fear of God" (Psalm 36:1; I Timothy 4:2). Through arrogance and depravity, the predisposition toward destruction has been established.

❦   ❦   ❦   ❦   ❦

Wounded and often feeling betrayed,
victims of child abuse and neglect
inevitably struggle with emotional intimacy
throughout their lives.

❦   ❦   ❦   ❦   ❦

Although God has made humans to be resilient, children cannot emotionally comprehend parental violations against them. Nor can their fragile emotions cope with yelling, screaming, hostility, and threats. At a time when children should be experiencing love and nurturing, betrayal and fear become their tormenting companions.

When children are abused, God has designed a method to keep their little souls intact. If you have read any recovery literature, you may be familiar with these terms: personality splitting, dissociation, emotional detachment, and hiding. These terms are used to describe a process whereby people are able to distance themselves emotionally from the trauma they are experiencing. Such distancing can occur after one painful incident or as the result of long–term, continuous abuse. One woman described it this way: "As my father was sexually abusing me, I seemed to step out of my body and could look down at him hurting me, but could feel nothing. I was numb." A male client, describing his reaction as a three–year–old to being abused, said he was able to "go away" inside of himself.

Victims who are able to recall the incidents or the feelings surrounding the abuse share a common denominator. The ability to develop emotional maturity has decreased and, for some, has been eliminated as a result of the trauma. Long after the violations have stopped and the perpetrator is gone, the wounded victim is unable to emotionally reconnect. Even as bodies and minds continue to develop over time, individuals are stuck emotionally, wounded and immature. Usually the victim finally seeks out help as a result of intense anger or depression.

Satan purposely targets the hearts and souls of small children because abuse is the most destructive weapon he can use to harm them. During formative development, young hearts and minds are greatly influenced by the events and messages they experience. Being immature and incapable of rationally analyzing their experiences, children concretely accept the distortions of abuse as fact. In addition, Satan knows that the lessons learned in childhood are difficult to root out, even if they are exposed later in life. Consequently, if he is able to wreak havoc on the hearts and souls of little children in such a way as to neutralize their ability to trust or risk relationally, he has won. Wounded and often feeling betrayed, victims of child abuse and neglect inevitably struggle with emotional intimacy throughout their lives.

The process of undermining the destinies of God's children is subtle and often missed by those involved. The outcomes, however, are obvious. Because children have not developed the resources or maturity to cope with abuse, they generally are unable to understand or work through the violations against them. If the abuse has been perpetrated by someone relationally close to the child, the damage and distortions to the abused child are often more severe than if the perpetrator is not related.

Likewise, since developing children view all experiences as somehow directly tied to their egocentric world, they often wrongly conclude that the abusive treatment is a result of their own "badness," and not of the abuser's lack of self–control. For instance, many parents shame their children by saying, "Bad boy!" or "You're a naughty girl!" To an adult, these words may mean very little, but such angry words always leave an imprint on the child's developing self–image.

How would it feel to be grabbed, yelled at, and shaken for doing something you really didn't understand? Even as an adult, with advanced cognitive capabilities, you might fail to grasp the reason for such treatment. Occasional shaming words are damaging, but not nearly as pervasive as ongoing physical, emotional, and sexual abuse.

Feeling "bad" and not understanding why God does not stop the abuse, the child concludes that God also believes he/she is bad and therefore does not love him/her. This creates internal confusion and self–devaluation. Feeling rejected and fearful, the child learns to distrust everyone, especially those he/she should be able to depend on. To escape painful feelings of badness and reality, the child creates an internal fantasy world that is safe, though often described as sad and lonely.

Adult victims who were not exposed to Christianity in childhood confess a bitterness that God did not protect them and therefore generally do not and cannot open their hearts to Him. Some victims have shared the experience of clinging to Jesus during childhood abuse and being comforted by Him in their make–believe world. As adult Christians they learn to embrace rules but not relationships. They guess at "normal behavior" by watching others and desperately try to "get it right," hoping to earn God's love, which they do not feel. Believing they are inadequate and emotionally immature, these victims grow up introspective and fearful. They seldom have the heart to share a faith with others that they do not feel themselves. Convinced that God is angry and hurtful like the people who abused them, they exhaust themselves trying to earn favor until they can no longer continue the pretense. Usually bitter and full of anger or self–hatred, they eventually either give up and turn away from religion or stay in church, emotionless and cynical.

❦ ❦ ❦ ❦ ❦

For most of us, the reasons we struggle
with emotional detachment and intimacy
are clear and can be found largely by examining
specific areas of our
development in childhood.

❦ ❦ ❦ ❦ ❦

Satan hates Christians because they are a reflection of God's glory. Christians represent the fruit of God's powerful salvation and victory over death through Christ. Still operating under the cloak of self–deception, the enemy continues to strike at the heel of God by attempting to steal those He loves from His hand.

For the most part, the adult victim of child abuse does not understand the underlying demonic scheme. However, the result is clear. When Satan is able through abuse or neglect to destroy the hearts of young children during their formative development, those children tend for the most part to grow up lifeless and to have great difficulty embracing God or His great salvation. They often lack a passion for the gospel that would compel them to reach out to others. Rather, they tend to hide from any personal disclosure about themselves and hope that their meager faith is enough to get them to heaven. They become masters of disguise and strive relentlessly to feel better about themselves. Often perfectionists, adult victims hide from the very thing they need most—the Lord's love. Sadly, once they begin to learn that they no longer have to be victims, they spend several more years wading through murky waters of self-focused recovery.

The answers are not black or white, nor are they grey. God has a full spectrum of bright and cheerful colors that represent His rainbow of healing. The Lord who created us is the very One we need to restore the damage done to our souls. David mirrored this very thought in the twenty-third psalm: "The Lord is my Shepherd,...He restores my soul...Even though I walk through the valley of the shadow of death, I will fear no evil, for you are with me; your rod and your staff, they comfort me."

Ultimately, we have to confront the lies we have believed and embrace the truth. Once we are able to get past our pain and grasp the truth in our hearts, the ripples of freedom begin to well up inside like a wonderful, warm spring that soothes and comforts.

In Ephesians 6:10–11, we are told to be "strong in the Lord and in his mighty power. Put on the full armor of God so that you can take your stand against the devil's schemes." In II Corinthians 2:11, Paul proclaims that "we are not unaware of his (Satan's) schemes." Let's open our eyes to truth and ask God to show us how Satan has damaged our souls. Let us then endeavor to take back the territory of our hearts that the enemy has stolen and commit ourselves to believe and to practice truth.

Our message must be the same as the Lord's. Forgiveness is there for those who are willing to repent of and make amends for the damage they have inflicted on others. God's desire is that we be reconciled to Him, to those we have wounded, and to those who have caused us to suffer (Romans 4:4–8; 5:10; Matthew 5:23; 18:15–20). The gravest offenses can be forgiven by the wounded child of God who understands the price Jesus paid for our sins (Matthew 18:21–35).

For most of us, the reasons we struggle with emotional detachment and intimacy are clear and can be found largely by examining specific areas of our development in childhood. God designed most of His creation to go through a process of stage–related growth. Whether it is a flower blossoming or a butterfly emerging from a cocoon, it is God's master plan that we all develop in a systematic way. If traumatic events inhibit a child from learning the skills necessary at various stages, the child's growth is impeded, sometimes indefinitely.

Begin to think about your childhood and ask yourself these questions. Did I learn the tasks I needed to in order to mature? Was there trauma that may have stalled my emotional growth? Am I still trying to get needs met that should have provided when I was a child?

As you grow in your understanding of child development, it is hoped that you will be able to return to the point at which you emotionally derailed and relearn what God intended you to experience the first time around. If you decide to venture down this pathway, be aware that the journey you are about to take will be bumpy, but it will be wonderful as you grow in the joy and security that come from being dependent on God.

Chapter 3

Understanding
How Children Develop

"I made you grow like a plant of the field.
You grew up and developed
and became the most beautiful of jewels..."
Ezekiel 16:7

*I*n 1964, I was a nine–year–old growing up with three older siblings. My scholastic interests were just beginning to bud. The prospect of college was far removed from my narrow scope of reality, but I knew that junior high was right around the corner. So, in true visionary fashion, I borrowed my brother's Eighth–grade algebra book and decided to get a head start.

I felt great anticipation as I secretly stowed away with my brother's math book in my parents' room on the floor behind their bed. Initially, I was slightly concerned by the thickness of the thing, only because my readers were still twenty to thirty pages in length. The thought of being able to understand 150 pages of numbers gave me a third–grade rush.

A child's mind at times runs wild with imagination and dreams. Being able to separate fantasy from truth is an adult skill (or so I believed). Children are not limited to such boundaries. I had envisioned numerous times the ability to skillfully teach myself Eighth–grade math. There was nothing particularly alluring about this academic interest other than it was the thickest "big" schoolbook I could find. In true childlike fashion, I was quite sure I possessed the natural stuff to master this information, or any, for that matter.

As I opened the book, my anticipation quickly turned to despair. The words in the foreword were too difficult for me to sound out. Also, some of the symbols were unfamiliar to me. I could not teach myself, because I did not have the tools to do so. You can't imagine the discouragement I felt and the blow to my ego. Further, my sense of failure at not being able to comprehend the words and symbols significantly impacted my ability to learn math or reading skills for many years.

What happened that day in my parents' room? How could my brief encounter with Danny's math book have had such a significant influence on my mind, emotions, and decision–making process? The simplest answer is that I tried to learn a skill I was not adequately prepared to master. To succeed at

Eighth–grade math, I needed four more years of progressive instruction in math foundations. In addition, I was not emotionally mature enough to cope with the "self–talk" message that I was "stupid" and "a failure." Nor had I developed the cognitive tools to analyze or rationally evaluate what had happened. Consequently, my childmind concluded that I was inadequate and incapable of mastering math or reading, a belief that followed me for nearly two decades.

The purpose of this chapter is to explain how children develop and how that relates to the distortions they struggle with as adults. If we think about the concept generally, no doubt most of us would easily comprehend the principles. Unfortunately, we tend to look at events through the eyes of adulthood and experience, not through the fragile, less–developed, and limited abilities of child thinking and feeling. To grasp a greater understanding, let's look at development the way it actually happens through stages of growth.

In I Corinthians, Chapter 13, Paul draws a comparison:

"When I was a child, I talked like a child, I thought like a child, I reasoned like a child. When I became a man, I put childish ways behind me" (vs.11). Later in the same letter to the Corinthians, Paul exhorts the believers to "stop thinking like children. In regard to evil be infants, but in your thinking be adults" (I Corinthians 14:20).

Children do not possess the same capabilities as adults and are not able to talk, think, or reason with adult maturity. How do we develop the ability to think and reason rationally as well as to feel and behave in a healthy way? Is it something that just happens as our bodies grow and our minds collect more information? Do our hearts and emotions simply go along for the ride, automatically adjusting?

Imagine life as if it were a beautiful, shiny, red Corvette. When we go to the dealer's showroom, we can see the finished product, sitting there wearing a huge price tag. "Oh, what a gorgeous car," we say to ourselves. "It's worth the price!"

Was the Corvette always that beautiful? No, cars don't just pop out of thin air that way. To the contrary, the Corvette goes through an infant stage that requires a great deal of work and effort before it is transformed into a beautiful sports car. Whether the material used is fiberglass or steel, each Corvette is hand–fashioned by experts who know what the end result needs to be. As each worker faithfully carries out the designer's instructions for building this work of art, shortcuts and scrimping on parts are not allowed.

Most of us have seen film clips of auto assembly lines. From beginning to end, necessary parts are added to the frame, each in the required sequence. What would happen if the interior seats of our imaginary Corvette were added to the bare steel frame or the tires assembled before the brakes? How long would this car last if the gas tank were mistakenly connected to the radiator? What would happen if all of these horrible things actually occurred and the designer came into the showroom to view his creation? What would he say to the managers he had entrusted to reproduce his valuable investment?

"How could you do this to me?" he might yell. "Didn't I spend thousands of dollars teaching you how to carefully build my car? Why didn't you follow my instructions? Look at this mess! No one will want to look at this car, let alone buy it. Everyone will think it was my fault, but it's your fault because I gave you what you needed to build this car and you didn't follow my design!"

The automakers would lose their jobs if they operated independently of the designer's drawings and specifications. Additionally, one can only imagine the potential danger both to the buyer and to innocent bystanders should the red Corvette venture off the assembly line.

This is an extreme example of what could happen if the workers failed to carefully build the Corvette according to the designer's intentions. We can take this same scenario and compare it to a child who experiences severe abuse or maltreatment in early childhood. Fortunately, most of us cannot relate to the severity of this illustration. It is hoped that a child being so blatantly abused by primary caregivers would be removed from the home long before reaching adulthood and offered help to restore the damage inflicted on God's precious little design. Jeremiah recorded the Master Creator's agony when His "unfaithful people" had sacrificed their children on the altar of idolatry and noted that they had done things He had never commanded and behaved in ways that had never entered His mind (Jeremiah 3:24–25; 7:31).

If we examine how a child develops, we can draw some startling similarities. A baby comes into the world dependent on primary caregivers. Awkward and needy, he or she can thrive only if cared for physically and emotionally. Similar to the red Corvette, a child learns and develops in a systematic way that blends the visible with the invisible into a whole person including physical, mental, emotional, and spiritual elements. The process goes on indefinitely, each element intermingling with the rest in a cumulative effort to carefully recreate the Master Designer's intent.

ã̃   ã̃   ã̃   ã̃   ã̃

Developmental psychologists believe that as much as 85 percent of a child's personality is formed by age seven. This means that most of what children believe about life and relationships has taken shape before they are ten years old.

ã̃   ã̃   ã̃   ã̃   ã̃

What happens if during the early stages of development the child experiences trauma related to physical, sexual, or emotional abuse? In most cases, especially those where external wounding is not permanent, it is often difficult to comprehend the variety of internal reactions that may result from the abuse. In other words, if your arm is broken, we can visually understand your discomfort and limitations. If your heart and soul have been damaged and we did not observe the offenses, empathizing with your pain becomes more challenging.

As an adult, you may still struggle with reactions tied to past woundedness and not be able to make the connection at all. The solutions are tied to understanding the developmental process. The preceding illustrations are intended to draw out several critical points as discussed in the following sections.

Children Grow in Stages

A baby emerges from a warm, safe place absolutely dependent. Every aspect of the infant's existence is controlled by someone else, usually the parents. Feeling safe and being dependent encompass the sum total of life.

As the child grows, the mind, body, emotions, and spirit respond to a continual stream of information. To successfully mature into a toddler, an infant has to learn several skills in each of these areas. Cognitively, the child begins to recognize and then place environmental objects into primitive groupings that eventually carry meaning. For instance, a new infant easily demonstrates a startle reflex because the information being received is unrecognized. An infant's initial responses are largely due to a cognitive inability to recognize and group information. Later, after observing, feeling, and experiencing the same people over and over, the child is able to begin the long process of growing intellectually.

Feeling safe is important for infants and small children because they lack the ability to take care of themselves. Being protected by and dependent on a loving parent or caretaker sets the foundation for future relationships. A safe and nurturing environment teaches a small baby that his/her world is basically good and trustworthy.

Negative experiences that produce serious wounding inhibit healthy development and growth. This is one reason that abused children create fantasy images in their minds about their parents or families in general. A child's mind is not developed enough to understand that parental abuse is the result of parental problems. Children tend to think (because that's what they are taught) that adults are always right. Therefore, they reason, if my daddy or mommy abuses me, I must be bad and deserve it. The thought produces shame and self–contempt in the heart of a child who longs to experience love and acceptance from his/her parents.

Understanding Core Beliefs

A child comes into the world an empty little vessel, ready to be filled with information and experiences. Developmental psychologists believe that as much as 85 percent of a child's personality is formed by age seven. This means that most of what children believe about life and relationships has taken shape before they are ten years old.

These early years are also the time when children are the least developmentally mature and the most susceptible to lies, distortions, and deception. Most children do not develop the ability to accurately analyze information cognitively until they are between the ages of eleven and fifteen.

Noted child psychologist Jean Piaget coined the term *concrete thinking* to accurately describe what children do. No doubt we've all experienced the stubborn little person who refuses to believe there are no monsters under the bed or ghosts in the closet. Part of the difficulty of getting children to believe what you are telling them is their intellectual and emotional immaturity.

Core beliefs are foundational values that we embrace as fact. For instance, if your mom or dad told you repeatedly as a small child that you were stupid, chances are better than not that in specific areas of your life as an adult you think it's true. Many individuals who hold postgraduate degrees and have been successful by every other standard are nevertheless stuck with such ludicrous ideas about themselves. Core beliefs are seldom rational, but they are always powerful!

Figure One illustrates the impact of core beliefs on a child's behavior, thoughts, and feelings. The left side of the graph demonstrates the extreme position of negative parenting and the far right a healthy parenting experience. Most of us have not experienced either extreme and probably fall somewhere in the middle. To determine which core beliefs rule you, circle the ones you most closely identify with.

Point of Reference

To accurately analyze or evaluate information, an individual must experience a stable point of reference. This means he/she has learned what is correct or reliable and can compare the current situation with a standard already recorded in his/her memory. Most children do not naturally possess this information and must be taught.

When abuse occurs before the age of ten, children have at

BEHAVIOR

This is what people see

This is what goes on inside

Abusive Childhood	**CORE BELIEF CONTINUUIM**	Healthy Childhood

I can not believe in my heart ....I do believe in my heart
God is not good and does not care ....God is good and He does care
I have no goals...I'm working on goals
I don't have longings or desires ....I have longings and desires
Isolation is the only way ....I'm connected relationally
I don't care about anyone ....I care deeply about others
I deserve to suffer ....**THOUGHTS**..................My life is precious
What's the point? ....I have a destiny
I am not loved ....I am loved
I am bad................................**FEELINGS**................I am good
I am betrayed ....I can trust
I am rejected...I am accepted
Life is not safe ....**DEEPEST CORE BELIEFS**....................Life is safe
People are not safe ....People are safe

their mental disposal only the information they have acquired to that point. If Mom or Dad or anyone else abuses them, they do not have the ability to recall a correct response, since they have never learned one. Instead, they develop a core belief that abuse is normal, and that belief becomes the standard by which they compare experiences. Of course, this has a horrible emotional impact on children, because at a time when they need to learn that for the most part their world is safe and trustworthy, they are experiencing just the opposite. Because of the pain they feel and the confusion that often follows, they usually conclude that people are not safe, their environment is not safe, and, therefore, nothing is safe.

If this conclusion is drawn by children during their formative years, they will most likely become stuck believing the messages they have learned. Although they continue to grow intellectually, physically, and, to a certain degree, spiritually, their ability to mature emotionally is stunted. The consequence is that these children grow up with numerous unmet needs. Not having a healthy foundation to build upon, they stay hidden and fearful long after the danger is gone. Well–developed self–protection mechanisms keep them from opening their heart and soul to anyone, including the Lord.

Haven't you met people who confess an inability to be emotionally vulnerable with even close friends or spouses? This same inability is seen in their relationship with God. How frustrating it is for believers who know theoretically that God is good and loving but who are stuck in their heart believing that He is really mean or that He doesn't love them because He didn't protect them from the abuse! This is a child's distortion based on a child's experience. Children often believe that since God is not safe, they dare not be dependent on Him or look to Him for help.

Mastering Specific Skills

Each developmental stage brings the ability to learn new

tasks and skills. Failure to learn the necessary skills because of neglect or abuse results in an inability to mature in the deprived areas. For instance, a child who injures an arm or a leg and does not use it will develop muscular atrophy. Intellectually, deprivation of mental stimulation can result in retarded growth, or what we might call brain atrophy. Spiritual atrophy may result when wounding produces an inability to practice what has been taught from Scripture or modeled by caregivers. As adults, these wounded souls may voice resentment as they recall a parent's preaching one thing but practicing another.

While it is more difficult to measure what might be called emotional atrophy, the evidence can be seen most easily in relationships. Victims of childhood abuse or neglect persistently avoid emotional closeness and have no concept of emotional intimacy. They are not able to give what they have not received, and they may doubt that such intimacy exists outside of movies and romantic novels.

Have you ever seen a five–month–old baby walk? Can a nursing infant look up at its mother and say, "Hi Mom, good meal!" Have you ever heard of a one–year–old who could recite the twenty–third psalm? The chances of such children performing the tasks mentioned would be pretty slim. Indeed, any parent knows that children learn with practice, practice, practice. You cannot run until you learn to walk. It's not possible to recite the twenty–third psalm until the cognitive ability is developed to properly group information and understand words and concepts.

Infants don't talk, because they haven't learned the specific skills needed to speak. In the emotional arena, the same holds true. To venture out relationally or otherwise, a child must learn to trust. A great deal of research suggests that failure to learn to trust before the age of two can result in severe damage to a child's ability to mature emotionally. Drawing the conclusion that the world is not safe results in the child's withdrawing and erecting self–protective barriers that keep people and pain out.

At a time when they should be exploring the world with excitement and curiosity, they are preoccupied with surveying their territory for signs of threat. Fear–based child development always produces emotionally immature adults.

While any form of abuse will inhibit emotional growth, neglect has a negative impact on development in a more subtle way. One victim recalls, "My parents didn't beat me. I wasn't abused physically or sexually. No one called me names or made me feel ashamed. For years, I could not understand why I felt like a 'nonperson.' But then I learned about passive abuse. I was one of seven children. I guess by the time my parents had me, there was nothing left. Neither of my parents ever held me or talked to me. My sister was kind of a mom, but mostly I was just alone. I feel like I drifted through life with no real sense of value or desire. Everything just seemed empty. Basically, I thought the Lord felt the same way about me. I was just there. It didn't matter one way or the other if I was around as long as I kept out of the way."

The term *passive abuse* implies that the parent(s) failed to provide the necessary nurturing and care needed for the child to grow and develop emotionally. Such failure can result in emotional damage, much the same as the child who is not provided food, clothing, learning opportunities, etc. Personal oversight by and interaction with parents are critical. Children need to learn life principles and skills through parental involvement, not through television and peers.

We often fail to understand emotions because we can't see them. The results of neglect and abuse are often misdiagnosed or unrecognized at all until something terrible occurs that forces acknowledgment of the problem. Common examples include acting out at school or home, bed–wetting, recurring nightmares, anger outbursts, and withdrawal. The skyrocketing incidence of teen suicide and depression is an ugly reminder that we have failed to give our kids what they need.

Unfortunately, the secular world has been more than happy to make up for the neglect of the Christian community by providing a constant stream of immorality and temptation packaged in socially acceptable and desirable messages. The church is largely seen as ineffective and boring compared with the promises of love, happiness, and success offered by the mass media. The only price is compromise!

But we were not taught, and have not passed on, a healthy and godly standard by which to compare these messages. Children more often than not will give in to what they are experiencing. Worse, if we learned hypocrisy and teach it to our kids, it is inevitable that they not only will hate our double standards but also will, in some distorted way, believe they are at least "being honest" about who they are. This conclusion is becoming commonplace amid the rubble of empty convictions.

Failure to Learn Age-specific Tasks

Not only do children fail to grow emotionally, but they deteriorate and accept core belief distortions about themselves, about what healthy relationships should be like, and about God. In a child's mind, parents are the same as God. If parents are abusive or neglectful, children conclude that God must also be abusive or neglectful. If Daddy was mean and harsh, then God must be that way, too. If Mommy is critical and demands perfection, children often believe that everyone in authority is like that. Such messages produce in children a desperate need to please. When a child's best efforts are met with ridicule or abuse, helplessness and despair set in, often resulting in resignation and feelings of failure.

❧   ❧   ❧   ❧   ❧

The detachment process occurs when children have reached the end of their ability to cope with pain, whatever the source.

❧   ❧   ❧   ❧   ❧

Generalized distortions learned in childhood unfortunately motivate many Christians. Unable to understand how to change inaccurate beliefs against their point of reference for what they think is normal, they hide behind a cloak of legalism, fearful of being exposed. Many simply live in a perpetual state of denial, refusing to acknowledge their contradictions. Honest feelings and convictions locked behind walls of confusion are finally released when the roots of the distortions are revealed. The immature concepts formed early in childhood erupt from the depths of the soul.

When children derail at one stage because they are unable to master the skills needed to go on to the next stage, they become stunted in that particular area. The missing element might be trust, risktaking, attachment, or feeling safe. Without mastering each element, the child constantly struggles with insecurity, fear, and a consequent reluctance to venture out into other territories, as would be the normal course of development.

Experiencing Severe Emotional Trauma

Our society seems strangely ambivalent toward children. On the one hand, we will empty our pockets and hearts at the sight of children's emaciated bodies on television and rise up in anger and indignation at the mere suggestion that these children would be abused. Yet we continue to ignore the statistics that say our own children's development is stunted daily as a result of maltreatment. With tougher legislation in place to discourage physical abuse, irresponsible parents have shifted to emotional and sexual abuse as their crime of choice. Slapping and assaulting has turned into yelling and intimidating. Using their size and authority, adults are mistreating children in record numbers and are threatening to further harm them if they tell.

Children are not designed to cope with abuse. They have no resilient quality that enables them to comprehend physical, sexual, or emotional violations against them. When abuse occurs, most children are able to survive by distancing themselves emotionally from the pain. Much like the person in shock when an arm is severed or who suffers amnesia when subjected to a traumatic event, a child victim often detaches emotionally or dissociates. This God–given defense mechanism helps the child survive the immediate trauma but can at the same time prevent the child from experiencing future emotionally nonthreatening situations.

The detachment process occurs when children have reached the end of their ability to cope with pain, whatever the source. This can come as the result of one horrifying incident, such as one incident of sexual abuse, or through less intense but prolonged, steady violations. Progressive detachment can occur in homes where parents are frequently angry and explosive, either at each other or at their children.

The children in such homes determine, sometimes unconsciously, that feelings hurt and therefore must be bad. Instead of learning to explore the wonderful world of emotions, they learn not to express their feelings. Confused and often bewildered by the insatiable needs inside them that long to be met through loving and nurturing relationships, they are stunted by fear and overwhelmed by their reality. Instead of maturing in their ability to give love and affection, children may cower behind a wall of pain and isolation, with elementary emotional skills left unlearned.

As the wounded child grows physically, his/her unmet needs become self–centered and unrelenting. Driven by conflicting motives, the adult child progresses through one relationship after another, always needing too much and unable to give enough. Desperately longing for something the child does not understand, the emotional emptiness renders the heart numb and distant, refusing to come to life on command. Eventually, the embarrassed adult tires of the battle and resigns him/herself to a life of emotional isolation and self–contempt.

To heal, a person must return to those places in his/her emotional development where trauma caused the derailment. Ultimately, where the person got off is where he/she has to get back on. Finding the location may be difficult to do alone, especially if childhood memories are sketchy or nonexistent, as is the case with many adult victims.

During the course of our journey, we will examine God's master plan as presented in Scripture. The purpose of doing so is to establish God's standard for the provision of physical needs, protection needs, and emotional–nurturing needs. The list is not comprehensive, but it does cover major areas often cited in therapy involving abuse.

The Scriptures chosen that best represent each category will be examined for both practical and spiritual application. Since God Himself designed us with specific needs, He is always aware of our dilemma of how to meet those needs in a fallen world. He understands the complexity of our pain. He who formed us in His image is also the one David speaks of in Psalm 71:5–6:

> *"Lord God, you are my hope.*
>
> *I have trusted you since I was young.*
>
> *I have depended on you since I was born.*
>
> *You have been my help since the day I was born.*
>
> *I will always praise you."*

Practical Exercises

1. What were the major core beliefs you developed as a child in relation to
   a. Safety

   b. Trust

   c. Dependency

   d. Feelings

2. Do you remember dissociating because of severe physical, mental, sexual, emotional, or spiritual pain or trauma? Can you give specific examples?

3. Did you feel free to grow and develop as a child? If not, what were some of the reasons?

4. What did you learn about God as a child? Whom did you primarily learn from? Was God talked about in your household when you were growing up? If so, can you remember in what context?

5. Who did most of the instructing in your home—your father or your mother? What kinds of skills did you learn without your parents' help? Were there things you would have liked their help with?

Chapter 4

Understanding How Children Learn

"Now, Israel, listen to the laws and commands
I will teach you. Obey them so you will live...
Don't add to these commands.
And don't leave anything out.
But obey the commands of the Lord your God
that I give you...be careful!
Don't forget the things that you have seen.
Don't forget them as long as you live.
Teach them to your children and grandchildren...
Then they will respect me
as long as they live in the land.
And they will teach these things
to their children...."
Deuteronomy 4:1–2,9–10

The instruction that God gave through Moses in the desert was designed to establish a divine bond of dependency between the Lord and His people. Far from being impersonally involved, God would tenderly provide His children with all they needed to know about His ways, character, and great love for them. To ensure continued familial intimacy, the Lord repeatedly instructed the Israelites to carefully and accurately pass on all that He would teach them. In so doing, they would reap the rich benefits He had joyfully created for them.

In the previous chapter, we looked at the way children develop. We will now focus on the intricate process of learning. As a basic security need, godly teaching and example by parents who love and obey the Lord are essential for healthy living. The clearest picture of this can be seen in Scripture. While men were at times presented as aggressive, ruthless, and scheming, they were also portrayed as tender, protective, and responsible in their actions toward God and those He had given to them. Honor and responsibility went hand in hand.

❧ ❧ ❧ ❧ ❧

The failure to pass on in detail God's ways, His character, and His heart has resulted in successive generations who choose to obtain their religion at the corner bookstore, where the price is cheap and little is required of the purchaser.

❧ ❧ ❧ ❧ ❧

In the past, even though marriages were generally arranged by parents and conceivably lacked the heart connection many of us deem valuable in today's society, God's people practiced an ethic that placed great importance on parenting in the ways of the Lord. Maintaining a strong Judeo belief system required that parents pass from one generation to the next the mighty workings of their benevolent God.

God taught life principles that would result in good physical health, prosperity, and loving relationships. Clearly, Scripture is full of how–to principles for parenting that provide the foundation for creating a long, satisfying life. God's architectural design for dependency has always been an integral part of His master plan.

Instruction as a requirement for growth sets a premise that children can be secure if they develop a clear, consistent belief system that they are able to follow. Likewise, it recognizes that what children learn during their early years is what they hold onto as adults. Parental teaching and a lifestyle that rightly reflects and represents God are critical to healthy growth and child development.

This master plan the Lord established can be seen throughout Scripture. God began the building with a foundation of truth. Through the Ten Commandments, He set a mandate for how His children should relate to Him and to others. Later, He added bricks of moral principle that would provide not only direction but also consequences if violated (Deuteronomy 28). He knew that weak or compromised bricks if left undetected could and would tumble a building to the ground. Thus, the Lord graciously provided the recipe for solid bricklaying. If followed, the house would withstand even the worst of life's storms; if compromised, the sturdiest house would crumble under the weight of the burden (Matthew 7:24–27).

The failure to pass on in detail God's ways, His character, and His heart has resulted in successive generations who choose to obtain their religion at the corner bookstore, where the price is cheap and little is required of the purchaser. Built on traditions of compromise and neglect, the bricks made of sand, many of which represent the self–centered values of our own choosing, have turned to rubble, beaten down by storms of disappointment and loss.

If we are to restore Christian and family values as taught by God, we must be committed to obeying Scripture and following biblical principles and instruction. In addition, we must once again embrace in the depths of our hearts the emotional fervor and passion that captivated God's people for centuries.

Let's now examine how children learn, particularly as learning relates to the development of core beliefs. Scripture supports two major concepts in relation to the teaching of children. First, we see God personally instructing parents and then providing guidance and oversight. Second, we see parents being instructed to follow God's example. As children grow, many others contribute to their overall learning experience, but always the direct relationship between God and parent and then between parent and child is perceived as the fundamental norm.

In the first category,—God Teaching His Children—we see the perfect example of God demonstrating the character traits we have been discussing. In an expression of love and intimacy, King David wrote of his dependent need of God's instruction:

Lord, I give myself to you. My God, I trust you.

Lord, tell me your ways. Show me how to live.

Guide me in your truth. Teach me, my God, my Savior.

I trust you all day long...The Lord is good and right.

He points sinners to the right way.

He shows those who are not proud how to do right.

He teaches them his ways.

All the Lord's ways are loving and true for those

who follow the demands of his agreement...

Is there someone who worships the Lord?

The Lord will point him to the best way.

He will enjoy a good life.

His children will inherit the land
Psalm 25: 1–2,4–5,8–10,12

Humility is an essential quality that one must possess to

experience God's mercy and direction. Although this virtue is mocked in contemporary society because it contradicts the popular value placed on pride and self–reliance, Solomon, David's son, learned that humility comes before honor (Proverbs 15:33; 18:12). The fear (or respect) of the Lord—which suggests willing submission—is critical to all that is truly meaningful.

We next see the important biblical principle of Parents Teaching Their Children that which they have learned from the Lord (Psalm 44). The major responsibility for the education of children is placed on fathers (Deuteronomy 4 and 6, Proverbs 4), although several passages encourage children to likewise listen to the instruction of their mothers (Proverbs 31:1,26; 30:17; 1:8).

In Ephesians 6:4, Paul writes, "Fathers, do not make your children angry, but raise them with the training and teaching of the Lord." This principle had been given to Paul through a rich tradition that emphasized God's love and authority. Second Timothy 3:15 tells us that children are to begin learning about the Lord as infants. The clearest biblical indication of the transfer of godly instruction throughout the ages can be gleaned from Psalm 78:1–8,10:

> *My people, listen to my teaching. Listen to what I say.*
>
> *I will speak using stories. I will tell things*
>
> *that have been secret since long ago.*
>
> *We have heard them and know them.*
>
> *Our fathers told them to us.*
>
> *We will not keep them from our children.*
>
> *We will tell those who come later*
>
> *about the praises of the Lord.*
>
> *We will tell about his power*
>
> *and the miracles he has done.*
>
> *The Lord made an agreement with Jacob.*

He gave the teachings to Israel.
And he commanded our ancestors
to teach them to their children.
Then their children would know them,
even their children not yet born.
And they would tell their children.
So they would all trust God.
They would not forget what God had done.
Instead, they would obey his commands.
They would not be like their ancestors
who were stubborn and disobedient.
Their hearts were not loyal to God.
They were not true to him...
They didn't keep their agreement with God.
They refused to live by his teachings.

Exodus and many of the other Old Testament books appear to have a consistent theme. When the Israelites were obedient and kept the Lord's instruction and loving acts on their lips, repeating them to each generation, the people walked with the Lord faithfully and were free from their enemies. Likewise, when they forgot the Lord and compromised His laws and principles, one generation after another turned away from God and ignored the paths of goodness that had resulted in blessing and peace (Psalm 49). The consequence of disowning the Lord or maintaining only lip service was that the children were reared as religiously legalistic or completely ungodly (Isaiah 29:13; Matthew 15:8; I Samuel 2:12; 3:11–13).

By design, fathers are to raise their children to experience God's goodness through them and to learn firsthand what happens to the family that prays together. The children in such a family will develop a maturity that will motivate them to grow and continue to learn God's ways long after they have left home. Modeling is important. In the same way that God promised to guide His people by example (Exodus 13:21; Psalm 25:9; Isaiah 58:11), human fathers are responsible for demonstrating the qualities their children are to emulate (Proverbs 4:11; Psalms 34:11; 37:25–28).

When we consider that a child's personality and beliefs are formed for the most part by the age of ten, we must recognize that the child's learning experiences during that period of development are critical. While it is true that behaviors and beliefs can be modified after that age, attempting to do so is the equivalent of trying to push a car uphill! To demonstrate the kinds of problems that can emerge as a result of formative inconsistency, let's examine Michael's story.

Michael was born into a family of working–class parents. His father had been reared in an alcoholic home, where Michael's grandfather drank away the family's modest income and his grandmother faithfully took the children to Bible school.

Although he was often drunk and seldom at home, Michael's grandfather seemed to have a warm, open heart toward his children. On the other hand, his grandmother was cold and distant toward her husband and their offspring. Tired of carrying all the responsibility for parenting and bitter at her husband's squandering of their meager resources, Michael's grandmother had been physically and emotionally abusive to her children. The Lord's name was heard often in this small, crowded household, but usually in the form of cussing. The children grew up confused by the many inconsistencies in their home. Dad was irresponsible, but warm; Mom was religious and bitter. The result of the mixed messages could be seen in each of the six children.

The eldest son grew up to become a hard–working alcoholic. The two oldest daughters married men who drank too much and chased after other women. The fourth child became a preacher, but seldom visited any of his family. The third daughter never married at all and pursued a career in business. The youngest son was Michael's father, a strange blend of both his parents. Quiet and friendly like his father, he had followed in his father's footsteps and had taken on the family shop. Lurking below the surface, however, was an angry man who demonstrated his hatred of women through passive–aggressive behavior.

Michael's mother was a mirror of his grandmother. She was angry and controlling but rigidly adhered to her family's religion. In addition to criticizing her husband's every move and embarrassing him in front of the children, Michael's mother was also prone toward depressive episodes where she would swear and yell and then cry and beg for forgiveness.

❦   ❦   ❦   ❦   ❦

Being able to understand where and how
we learned the core beliefs that drive us
is the first step in altering faulty values,
distortions, and inappropriate behavior.

❦   ❦   ❦   ❦   ❦

From the age of five, Michael went to church every Sunday. He saw his parents secretly put out their cigarettes just before entering the sanctuary and regularly had his mouth washed out with soap for using cuss words he had learned from them. The golden rule in his home was "Do as I say, not as I do," as Michael experienced a steady diet of God's wrath and punishment through his bitter mother.

The confusing message to Michael was that daddies are nicer, but they don't go to church much, and mommies are more religious, but they are also mean. Michael knew that his father would do anything for him, especially if it crossed his mother's authority. The continual frustrations of living with a distant husband had led Michael's mother to use shame tactics on her husband. By the time he left home, Michael had learned to respect his compromising father and to resent his religious but cold mother.

Just like his parents, Michael grew up with mixed values and an internal uncertainty about God, about what parents are, and, ultimately, about who he was. As a young adult, he found it difficult not to practice what he had learned. A chameleon in many ways, Michael's friendly and accepting disposition led associates at work and in his church to see him as a wonderful and deeply spiritual man.

At home, the picture was different. The glued–on smile that warmed the hearts of his colleagues would quickly turn to a sneer when Michael entered his house. Michael's wife accused him of being a phoney—one way at home and a totally different way outside. She saw Michael as cold, indifferent, and preoccupied with maintaining his image at church and at work. She complained that Michael's facade would quickly drop whenever she attempted to get him to interact with her emotionally. In addition, while he was more than willing to spend time teaching Sunday school or leading the youth group, he refused to pray with his own children or to oversee their godly instruction.

We can see from Michael's family tree how generational behaviors and attitudes are passed on. In addition, by the time Michael married and had children, the combined dysfunction of his origin and that of his wife had resulted in a horror story. All their children grew up angry, confused, and defiant. Only one of them gave any lip service to Christianity. The rest of the children viewed God as being either like their compromising father or like their angry, bitter mom. In either case, they had concluded that they were better off without the confusion.

Scripture says it is better to not have known the ways of righteousness than to have known them and then turn away (II Peter 2:17–22; Hebrews 6:1–6). When children early in life learn a distorted brand of Christianity that is compromised and inaccurate, the impact is far–reaching, with each successive generation falling further away from the truth of the gospel.

Many of us struggle because we have never seen untainted Christianity. Our perceptions of God have been colored by the character of those who raised us. Changing these perceptions is difficult because of the core beliefs we have developed by imitation and formative learning.

The easiest people to convert to Christianity are often those who have never heard the gospel. In Western countries where children have been, for the most part, exposed to a compromised version of God's eternal message, people tend to have a tremendous hardness of heart.

As we endeavor to journey backward toward God's initial design, let's try to put into perspective the messages we learned during our childhood. To do that, we must commit ourselves to accept the truth of God as revealed in Scripture and to compare our child learning experiences with God's standard. Being able to understand where and how we learned the core beliefs that drive us is the first step in altering faulty values, distortions, and inappropriate behavior.

Take your time to review the things you learned in childhood. Record in a journal or notebook the character traits you saw in your parents or caretakers. Then try to compare your own character traits with theirs. For instance, if your father was a friendly, generous man who was optimistic and vulnerable, are you that way, too? Was either of your parents angry or bitter? Did your parents pray with you every night? Were they warm and accepting? Was there underlying anger or tension in your home?

Many of us tend to fear that we will become like the parent we had the most difficulty getting along with. This is common in family dynamics. Try to be open and honest about your life and your childhood. If your experience of family differs significantly from that of your siblings, you may want to review it. Sometimes when we are unhappy as children, we create a memory of a better family than is really true. In chapter 6, you'll meet Jessie and be able to see how her make–believe family developed over time as a result of abusive and negligent parenting.

To honestly appreciate dependency on God, we will have to grapple with our family of origin (the people who raised us) and be willing to rethink our experiences. The value in working through unresolved issues from our past is that we are able to finally grieve the losses and release the pain of the wounds that have been festering for so long. In so doing, a freedom and openness results that allows a truly intimate relationship with the Lord and others to flourish.

Now, let's go on! The first stop on our journey home to revisit childhood memories will be to examine physical security needs. This is an area most of us take for granted, but it can become the foundation stone of uncertainty in our lives if we were abused or neglected and can impact our most basic belief about God's goodness.

Practical Exercises

1. What were the major core beliefs you learned in child-hood about
a. What a daddy does?

b. What a mommy does?

c. Who you were?

2. In what areas did your father and mother provide per-sonal instruction and oversight to you?

3. In what ways do you perceive of God as being like
a. Your father?

b. Your mother?

4. What did you learn in childhood about God? Jesus? What they are like?

5. Did you believe as a child that God cared about your needs and feelings?

6. How did you learn about relationships as a child?

7. Did either of your parents teach you godly character traits by their example? If yes, in which areas? If not, did anyone teach you about godly character?

PART TWO

Understanding
The Journey

"So I tell you, don't worry about the food you need to live.
And don't worry about the clothes you need for your
body. Life is more important than food.
And the body is more important than clothes.
Look at the birds in the air.
They don't plant or harvest or store food in barns.
But your heavenly Father feeds the birds.
And you know that you are worth
much more than the birds.
You cannot add any time
to your life by worrying about it.

And why do you worry about clothes?
Look at the flowers in the field.
See how they grow. They don't work
or make clothes for themselves.

But I tell you that even Solomon
with his riches was not dressed
as beautifully as one of these flowers.
God clothes the grass in the field like that.
The grass is living today, but tomorrow
it is thrown into the fire to be burned.
So you can be even more sure
that God will clothe you.
Don't have so little faith!
Don't worry and say, 'What will we eat?'
or 'What will we drink?'
or 'What will we wear?'
All the people who don't know God
keep trying to get these things.
And your Father in heaven
knows that you need them.
The thing you should want most is
God's kingdom and doing what God wants.
Then all these other things
you need will be given to you.
So don't worry about tomorrow.
Each day has enough troubles of its own.
Tomorrow will have its own worries."
Matthew 6:25–34

Chapter 5

Physical Needs
A Matter of Provision

"I have learned to be satisfied
with the things I have
and with everything that happens.
I know how to live when I am poor.
And I know how to live when I have plenty.
I have learned the secret of being happy
at any time in everything that happens.
I have learned to be happy
when I have enough to eat
and when I do not have enough to eat.
I have learned to be happy
when I have all that I need
and when I do not have the things I need.
I can do all things through Christ
because he gives me strength."
Philippians 4:12–13

The topic of physical needs brings to mind the famous observation, "I complained because I had no shoes until I met a man who had no feet." We all have different perceptions of what it is to go without and what it means to have abundance. An individual's point of reference as framed in childhood is the foundation stone of that individual's belief system. If early experiences are healthy, one will most likely develop the ability to grow and blossom as God intended. On the other hand, if childhood included severe deprivation, the child may lack the consistency necessary for healthy development.

The next chapter examines what Scripture teaches about God's standard for the provision of housing, food/water, clothing, and health care. For each area, notice the practical and spiritual comparisons Jesus and the Father make. In the meantime, the rest of this chapter briefly describes man's standard with regard to these basic needs.

An individual's point of reference as framed in childhood is the foundation stone of that individual's belief system.

Housing is more than a roof attached to four walls. The provision of this important need has little to do with construction at all, but rather describes a certain kind of relationship. With an upward mobility mentality that sets its goals for bigger and better, people have sacrificed relationship for a structure. The decline of family cohesiveness is often connected to parents working out of the home more just to pay their mortgage. For others who moved from house to house and never established a sense of belonging, the idea of "home" carries no meaning at all. Food is a basic need that many people use in ways other than to sustain life. In your home, was food ever used as a replacement for intimacy or comfort? Did you observe Mom or Dad going for the ice cream or a beer after a fight? Was food used to reward or punish? In our society, the emphasis on food, whether it is "junk" or nutritious—and the obsessions that go along with it—captivate many of us in one way or another.

Clothing, once intended to cover our nakedness, is now more commonly used to reveal it! Billions of dollars are spent worldwide annually, cycling and recycling fashions to win friends and buy popularity. This is especially true among teenagers, who demand more and more money from their financially strapped parents just to keep up with their peers.

The health-care industry is becoming expensive, and many can no longer afford basic medical and dental coverage. Infant mortality rates are on the climb even in technologically sophisticated countries where help is available but less afford-able than in previous decades. The growing expense tied to life–saving medications and procedures has put insurance companies, physicians, employers, and the public at war with one another. Meanwhile, the quiet victims who have no voice are the poor and needy, who are often at highest risk. Children who grow up suffering from disabilities or diseases that could have been treated fight an internal war against bitterness.

Review your childhood experiences with God's standard or "plumbline" as revealed in Scripture. The messages you learned and the point of reference you developed from birth to the age of ten determined for the most part the core beliefs you value today. What are the areas in which you failed to receive a healthy point of reference?

Practical Exercises

1. In the area of physical provision, write down what you learned in childhood about

a. Housing (its importance, purpose, etc.)

b. Food/water

c. Clothing

d. Health care

2. In the areas listed in (1), do you struggle with problems related to deprivation, uncertainty, or excess? If yes, in what ways?

3. Do you feel anxious or fearful when you think about any area of physical provision?

4. As a child, did you feel confident that your parents would provide every need you had?

5. How did you feel about expressing needs to your parents?

Chapter 6

Housing, Food/Water, Clothing, Health Care

Tell the believers there to do these things
so that no one can say they are doing wrong.
A Believer should take care of his own relatives,
especially his own family.
If he does not do that, he has turned against the faith.
He is worse than a person who does not believe in God.
I Timothy 5:7-8

*J*essie appeared nervous and apprehensive when she came into my office. Her cautious eyes evaluated every inch of the room without the slightest movement of her head. Jessie was clearly uncomfortable and looked as if she would like to have been anywhere else. Undaunted by the forms she had to fill out and the questions I asked of her, Jessie's presentation of herself was flawless, as if she had prepared it beforehand. After confessing that it was her husband Gary who had insisted she come for counseling, Jessie began to describe his complaints.

"Gary says I am angry, sullen, overreactive, too sensitive, and snippy," Jessie stated somewhat matter-of-factly. "He thinks I need help, so here I am. But I'll tell you right now, I don't think his problem is me. I am much calmer than my parents ever were. I don't hit anyone. Rarely do I scream, and I come back and apologize within a couple of days every time I blow up. He's just too sensitive! I barely raise my voice and Gary walks out of the room. Also, he's too controlling. Has to have everything his way. So, I'm here because I said I would come one time. That's it. Go for it!"

Jessie basically felt that Gary was overstating her problems. As she compared her actions and reactions to the point of reference she had learned, Gary's criticisms seemed unfounded, especially in light of the experiences and deprivation Jessie had been exposed to as a child. As Gary continued to find fault with Jessie's communication style, Jessie found herself withdrawing from him even more. She was being conditioned by Gary's response. The more he criticized, the harder

---

- The responses in this and subsequent chapters that represent clients at various stages of childhood were largely gained through regression work in therapy, in which the clients were able to vividly recall specific feelings they had at different ages. To guard the integrity and intent of the feelings expressed, grammar and word usage have not been altered. It is hoped that this approach will make it easier to understand the progression and change that occurs over time.

she became. One year into their marriage, the young veteran of many domestic wars was wishing she had stayed single.

To better understand Jessie's core beliefs, let's take a quick journey through her life and relationships. Try to evaluate the conclusions Jessie drew as a child and how they affected her as an adult. Remember that although her experience is extreme, it is, unfortunately, not uncommon.

Core beliefs that Jessie developed during the formative period of her young life were still motivating her thirty years later. Despite having accepted the Lord at twenty–two, and having experienced a great deal of Christian training, Jessie could not see her problem. Occasionally, she felt concerned about her temper but believed that everyone must struggle with living in a fallen world. Since Jessie always compared her life and relationships with those of other people, she had decided that her issues were not as pronounced as many of those whom she respected in the church. Jessie was not able to comprehend that her behavior was only symptomatic of deeper things inside that were terribly amiss.

Jessie's Story

Jessie was five years old when her mother and father were divorced. Prior to the divorce, ongoing fights and escalating violence that often erupted at home caused the frightened little girl to disappear at the first sign of trouble. Far from running down the sidewalk to meet her father in the late afternoons, Jessie automatically kicked into a nervousness that mechanically directed her feet out the back door. Her mother also seemed to shift mindlessly into a defense mode around 4 p.m. daily, which usually meant Jessie would soon be in trouble. The younger siblings weren't old enough to understand or escape and tended to become whiny at the impending anger that would shatter their playful world.

This was life as Jessie knew it. Seldom had she seen her mother happy or her father relaxed and playful. Her parents both worried about things Jessie did not understand, like bills and clothes and groceries. Jessie often worried that their problems were because of her and her sisters. Maybe, the child reasoned, if they could be a little quieter or not cause problems, Mommy and Daddy would be happier. Jessie had tried to be good and had even stopped eating seconds at dinner, hoping to alleviate some of the reasons her parents fought.

Jessie at Age 3

> *"Mommy and Daddy are mad, mad, mad. They always fight. They fight and fight. Daddy say he tired of sweating all day. Mommy waste his money. He say we eating him out of house. I don't know what he mean. I eating less so Daddy not be mad ..."*

Jessie was not prepared for the adjustments that would be needed after her father left. A logger by trade, her father had been able to provide a dependable middle–class income until recent years. The economy had taken a downturn, and some of the older mills were being closed or renovated. Business and environmental concerns impacted the heart of the logging community and Jessie's family directly. As the debate in Congress heated up over closures, so did the ongoing wars at home. Fearing the inevitable, Jessie's mother had tried to get her husband to change careers, but he had refused. Finally, as the last blast of the whistle signaled the closing of the local mill, Jessie's parents announced an end to their stormy marriage.

Jessie at Age 5

> *"Mommy said Daddy is going away. He's angry. He yells all the time. Now Mommy says we are going to be alone. She says she will be nicer now. Daddy says Mommy is being mean to him. He is mean! I don't want him to go, sorta, but I don't like him to come home either. I don't know how we will make it. Daddy says we on our own. I hear him tell Mommy he's not going to send us money. He told Mommy we have to wear*

rags and starve now. Will my Daddy really let us starve? I'm scared. I don't sleep very well at night. I cry. I don't have anyone to talk to. Mommy is mad all the time. The babies need me to be happy."

Legal battles sapped the meager family savings. Then Jessie's father disappeared, with promises to send money after he found work. Left without a job or a husband, Jessie's mother had no alternative but to file for welfare.

Jessie at Age 8

"Today, I had to stand in a stinking line with creepy–looking people. They stunk! Mom looked straight ahead, like a zombie. I had a spinning head. Didn't know if someone might steal my purse. Won't get much. I got five cents. I don't like this! People look at us like we're icky scums. Why doesn't my dad help us? I don't want to be a poor person. Haven't had new shoes for a year. My toes are crunched and my toenails hurt. Mom says, 'Forget it.' Forget what? What's to forget? Life stinks like the line at welfare. It's getting worse and worse."

The changes came rapidly. First, the struggling family was evicted from their home and forced to live in a shelter. Jessie recalls the humiliation of standing in long welfare lines, waiting for food vouchers. The family moved from one low–income apartment to the next, always in seedy areas, where robberies occurred frequently. Each new incident caused Jessie to pull in a little tighter, clinging to the dream of someday being free from the growing emotional prison she found herself in.

Jessie at Age 11

"Dear Diary. You should see the new place we moved into! This time, I have a view of a garbage dump. Some of the garbage has legs. I'm sick of moving!!! Don't talk to kids at school anymore. No use. I leave. Kids look

at me funny. They say things about my clothes every day. Got sent to the principal three times this week for punching out creeps. They deserved it. How would they like it if I made fun of them? Told Mom about the teasing. She doesn't care. Yelled at me for gettin' in trouble. I yelled right back. She's stupid. Don't have any idea what pain she causes me. I found a pair of cool jeans today. I'm keepin' 'em. Can't tell Mom, though or she'll beat me. One of these days, I'm gonna beat her back. She don't care 'bout me. She just cares about her. Me and the girls have to take care of ourselves. Gonna have to find more lost clothes."

In an effort to bring in some extra money, Jessie's mother had found employment in a restaurant where the owner would pay her under the table. Jessie was required to help more with the house and children. This meant that she would miss several days of school each week to cover for her mother. Jessie bathed her sisters, put them to bed every night, and learned fifteen different ways to cook macaroni and cheese for meals.

At night she would listen to the police sirens outside her window and wonder if she knew the latest robbery victim. Jessie was a little girl stuck in an adult's world, with adult responsibilities. Weary from the battles, she would fall asleep curled up in a fetal position with her stuffed bunny—the one thing that was truly her own.

Far from being grateful that Jessie could take on so much, her mother was frustrated and her anger began to boil over at home. As if replaying her relationship with her husband, she looked for reasons to fight with Jessie.

Remembering that the winner is the one who yells the loudest and hits the hardest, Jessie often found herself in volatile struggles with her mother over little things. The fights were a way for her to vent the mounting effects of poverty and a means to blame someone else for the misery she was in.

Jessie at Age 12

"I hate her! I hate her! I am sick to death of her!

Someone get me out of here. I am tired! I am angry! I want out of here! Now!"

The physical security Jessie had known briefly as a young child was replaced with uncertainty and fear. As each month drew to an end, Jessie's mother recited her complaint that the children had not made the food last long enough. Unable to ration meals perfectly and refusing to accept responsibility for the problem, she would line the girls up and tell them how much trouble they were. Though the kids tried to be good, they were regularly informed that the state might send them away if their mother couldn't care for them any longer. The younger children would cry and run to their rooms to hide, but Jessie had learned to emotionally disappear during such outbursts.

As for dealing with her own hunger pangs, a neighbor lady had once told her that drinking lots of water with a few crackers would trick her stomach into thinking it was full. Though only thirteen, Jessie was well informed on all of the ways she could beat the system, even her physical condition.

Jessie at Age 13

"Dear Diary. Well, it was another rotten day. Mom gave us the usual stink about eating her out of house and home. She's a pig. Don't matter to me. The girls get sad and go cry. I stand there and look her down. She can't move me. She can't scare me. I'd love nothin' more than to go live somewhere else. The state can't be as bad as this! Anyway, maybe I'll get to live somewhere for more than a month. I can look at Mother and not hear her now. It's really cool. I did it to my teacher when he was mad at me. He thought I was listening politely, but I wasn't. I was at the circus, laughing at the fat lady..."

Apart from the regular struggles with her family, there were always concerns about their living situation. In one year, there had been four eviction notices and four trips to the shelter. There, Jessie was regularly exposed to down–and–out people who found their comfort in a bottle. It did not take long before she, too, became creative at using alcohol to numb her pain.

Having their power disconnected for nonpayment was a regular event. In the wintertime, the children would huddle in corners with blankets wrapped around them to keep from freezing. When they had power and a phone, Jessie would hear her mother yelling at the man who had abandoned them years before. Occasionally, Jessie's father would find them and promise to send money, which would make the girls watch the mailbox for days. But the letters from Daddy never came. Nor did he send the promised money. Having a phone was such a rarity in their house that the kids often fantasized that perhaps their daddy had tried to locate them and couldn't. It was not possible for them to comprehend why their daddy never came.

In school, the girls were learning that daddies are nice men who love their children and buy them nice things. They would wonder why *their* daddy wasn't like that, but the conclusions they came to weren't happy. In time, Jessie's little sisters made up a Daddy in their minds and would talk about him to the kids at school. After a while, they began to believe it.

Jessie lived for the day she could escape the lifeless, dreary existence she found herself in. Someday she would have a nice home, with lots of cupboards to fill with food. She was going to drive a fancy car and wear nice clothes, not like the rags she had been wearing for the past ten years. Jessie made a promise to herself never to trust anyone for anything. Streetwise at fifteen, she was a mother to her sisters, a maid, a student (sometimes), and always an angry young woman. Seldom would she talk to anyone about anything. As her anger began to turn inward, so did the health problems that followed.

Jessie at Age 15

"Dear Diary. I feel sick! Blah...blah... Told mother today about the blood. She told me to stop eating this and that. I've been more tired and my insides hurt. Mom says it's a little stress. Does stress make you bleed? It was really hard, but I asked her if I could go to the doctor. She said no. I told her I was going anyway. She said

*I couldn't without a voucher. I tried to take one out of
her purse, but she caught me, and we had it out. Went to
the nurse at school for somethin' to stop the pain. She
called somebody, somewhere, and they raised cain
with mother. Boy, did I get yelled at! Anyway, I got an
appointment now, but geez! It's a lot to go through to get
a little help!"*

After Jessie was finally allowed to see a physician, the tests
revealed a stomach ulcer. Jessie had to fight her mother constantly for the vouchers she needed to get medicine and to see
her doctor. Her mother had succeeded in carrying on a life of her
own through the years. Jessie's gifts and talents had been used
to take care of her sisters. Free from the burdens of reality,
Jessie's mother had sought out more pleasing environments.
When she did not work, she danced, dated, and visited friends.
Sometimes she came home at night; sometimes she didn't.
Searching for the childhood she never had, she robbed Jessie of
the one she needed to grow up strong. As if their roles had been
reversed, Jessie was old at sixteen, and her mother was young
at forty. The sisters were lost somewhere in the middle.

Let's look at the core beliefs Jessie struggled with as an
adult related to the provision of her physical needs. Remember
that core beliefs are those values we learned as a child that we
hold onto as an adult. As we examine Jessie's core beliefs, think
about your own upbringing. Do you see any similarities? It's
not essential to experience the same trauma or problems to
develop faulty values. Many of us lack healthy beliefs simply
because we were not taught them. We tend to develop the same
core values as those of our parents.

Sometimes these convictions are age appropriate, but
other times we get stuck believing inaccurate messages, no
matter how irrational they are. As we examine Jessie's story,
first note the beliefs Jessie expressed as a child. Then see how
her beliefs differ in her presentation as an adult.

Remember that children's perceptions of traumatic events
are what the children go by. If children have stalled emotionally

in specific areas because of severe wounding, they will not automatically mature in those areas. Many adults adjust or compensate by adopting the values or beliefs of others. Among Christians, the tendency is to accept theoretically the beliefs of pastors, teachers, or Bible study friends. As we become older, we pretend less and are more complacent.

Many who have not developed a healthy point of reference and who have not been exposed to recovery literature or groups seldom, if ever, evaluate their childhoods. If asked, they may conclude (after a lot of thought) that there was damage done but that they've managed better than a lot of people they know. Comparing dysfunction with worse dysfunction is not helpful. Such people are more likely than not to avoid conversation that would prompt them to look honestly at their feelings.

Give yourself permission to take the journey home for the purpose of evaluating your childhood against a biblical point of reference. See whether you can relate to any of Little Jessie's or Big Jessie's distortions, along with those you may have embraced.

Little Jessie's Core Beliefs regarding Physical Provision

Housing

"Home is a place where Mommy and Daddy fight and where little kids have to hide in fear. It is a scary place. When parents are around, you want to leave or you will get in trouble. Home is where you have to watch everything going on, because if you don't, bad things can happen. Home is not a safe place. It's not a place where you stay very long. You always have to leave because you don't have enough money. But that's okay, because the places are icky anyway. Don't matter where we live. It's going to be bad."

Food

"My friends say I'm poor, because I have bad lunches to take to school. I never know when we are going to run out of food. I get tired of the same old stuff, but I think about food all the time. I like to go to the neighbor lady's house to eat. I get two helpings or more. Once I ate so much I had to throw up."

Clothing

"Mommy says we have to shop at the Salvation Army for clothes. They smell funny, and people look at me like I am poor. Mommy picks icky clothes out and makes me wear clothes too big. She says I won't outgrow them. I don't like nobody to see me. I wish I could have shoes that fit. I feel so sad. Why don't my daddy take care of me? I used to have nice shoes. Now my toes hurt."

Health Care

"It's no good to get sick. There's no one to help. I got real sick with a cough and stuff. I had to go to school anyway. The nurse say I should be home in bed. Nobody there to take care of me. I might as well be here. Sometimes I have bad dreams that someone will hurt me. I don't know if anyone would help me."

Adult Jessie's Beliefs
Regarding Physical Provision

Housing

"It's not such a great thing to own a house. It's better to rent. With the economy the way it is and relationships the way they are, you wouldn't want to get stuck with something you couldn't unload. I don't care about houses, anyway. All I want is a good roof *over my head that doesn't leak and isn't embarrassing. We fight about buying a 'home'. Maybe someday I'll feel differently about it, but for now, I get nervous at the thought."*

Food

"All right, I admit that I like food a lot. Actually, it's kind of a love–hate thing. I love the idea of having lots of food available, and I keep my shelves packed. Gary teases me about having five kinds of cereal, tons of macaroni and cheese, and a pantry full of every form of culinary delight. Sometimes I want to keep eating, even when I'm full, but that's the way I am. I love food, but it doesn't love me. I had to finally join a gym and a diet club to keep the weight off. I feel really fat. Gary says I'm too skinny as it is, but he's crazy!"

Clothing

"And speaking of clothes, that's one problem. My sizes keep changing, and so does my wardrobe. I used to be so poor, I feel like I owe it to myself to shop. Gary thinks I have too many pairs of shoes. Maybe. It's true that I can line the room with them, but you never know when they might get uncomfortable. Mostly, I don't buy a lot. Shopping is a way of relaxing. It helps me unwind when I'm stressed out or when Gary and I have problems. It's harmless and a lot cheaper than drinking or smoking."

Health Care

"Gary and I were talking about the amount of Maalox I consume because of my ulcer. He thinks I'm a hypochondriac. It's not that. I have lots of health problems. I've had to have several surgeries. Gary thinks I'm a surgeon's bowl of cherries. That's ridiculous. I just

have had some bad health problems. It's good that I have insurance. I'm probably one of the few people who has gotten more out of the company than I've paid in. I like my doctor. She really cares about my problems."

❦ ❦ ❦ ❦ ❦

Often, the most erroneous beliefs come from Christians who have studied the word of God but have taken in only those Scriptures that fit their theology.

❦ ❦ ❦ ❦ ❦

Can you see the difference between Jessie's core beliefs as a child and those as an adult? Deep down, Jessie was terribly insecure and afraid to trust anything or anyone. Commitment had been a lifelong struggle for her. Living without depression or health problems was Jessie's greatest challenge. Jessie didn't care to engage in other activities and felt that she didn't have the energy anyway. What do you think God intended Jessie to experience as a flower in His beautiful garden?

Biblical Standard For Physical Provision

Although Jessie's perceptions with regard to her physical needs changed over time, God's never changed. His plan and purposes stand forever (Psalm 33:11) and are not altered by time or circumstances. But what are we to understand about our physical needs? Is God concerned about them? These questions are complicated because we intrinsically lack sufficient insight into all the dealings and purposes of our God. Since what we do know about God's plan is revealed through Scripture, our best hope for understanding the ways of God is hinged on our willingness to search the Scriptures, meditate on them, pray to God for insight, and live out the principles and instruction He has given to us.

Often, the most erroneous beliefs come from Christians who have studied the word of God but have taken in only those Scriptures that fit their theology. For instance, Jessie had found every passage in the Bible that proved to her that God is angry and violent. Her daddy had been mean, abusive, and perpetually raging during the few years she knew him. She was stuck in a belief that fathers are that way, even her Heavenly Father! It took months to persuade her of the truth.

As we went through one Scripture after another that painted Abba as a loving and just Daddy who always acts in our best interest (Isaiah 30:18–21; Psalm 36:5–10; I John 2:5; Psalm 103:4; Deuteronomy 1:31, etc.), I could see the obvious look of disbelief on Jessie's face. Time and again, I asked Jessie whether she believed Scripture was true. Her answer was usually, "Yes, but...." Jessie's view of God mirrored the feelings she had about her father and was stronger and more deeply etched in her soul than Scripture, which Jessie agreed was a better standard.

As we look at a few of the passages that deal with physical provision, you may confront the same reality warp! Specific verses may grate against your core beliefs. If that happens, take a few minutes to think about the reasons you are struggling with those passages. If the thinking trail takes you back to your childhood, don't be afraid to look at it honestly. The purpose of what I call the "journey home" is not to needlessly stir up the past, but to help correct distortions that impact relationships today. Keep in mind that it is our *perceptions* that are inaccurate, not God's word (Proverbs 30:5; II Samuel 22:31; Job 11:4; Psalm 18:30).

Let's begin by examining the spiritual applications that are relevant to our most basic areas of physical need. God is the Creator and Sustainer of all things (Genesis 14:19; Hebrews 1:3). Even members of the animal kingdom cry out to and receive food from the Father of life (Job 38:41; Psalm 147:9). As we look at God's design for human provision and His intimate role as YHWH (pronounced "Yahweh"), our Lord and Provider, let's consider six principles of God's standards for physical provision.

1. *Divine provision is tied to relationship with God.* God has a greater concern about our spiritual state than our physical well–being, although both are important to Him (Matthew 6:25–34; Deuteronomy 28, 1:31; Psalm 111:4–5; I Timothy 6:17; Proverbs 13:25, 10:3; Matthew 15:32–38; Romans 8:35–39; Luke 6:21; Psalm 146:7; Genesis 9:3; Exodus 23:25; Leviticus 26:3–5; Deuteronomy 10:17–18; Ruth 1:6; Psalm 65:9; Psalm 145:14–16; Luke 15:17–24; John 4:31–34; John 5:26–35; Acts 14:17; II Corinthians 9:10–11; Proverbs 49:10; John 6:48–51).

Jessie did not have a healthy relationship with her father and had not heard of God except when His name was used for cussing. The fact that her father had not provided for his family had taught Jessie that daddies could not be trusted to take care of her needs. Ultimately, she believed that no one cared for her and she would have to take care of herself. Self–reliance, not Jesus, had been her salvation as a child. As an adult, she had an ongoing struggle believing that God wanted to provide for any of her needs or that He loved her. Although she verbalized the belief that "Jesus loves me, this I know," she confided in therapy that she didn't buy it for a moment, at least not in relation to her.

Once Jessie began to realize that God had made an eternal home for her and that she would eventually forget the sadness of her past, she was able to begin releasing the feelings of rejection she had nurtured since childhood. Through Scripture, Jessie began to understand that Jesus does care about the little children and that He had cared about all her pain (Matthew 18:1–7; 19:13–15).

2. *It is possible to be in God's will and suffer homelessness, hunger, thirst, nakedness, and/or physical problems, although this is rarely the case for believers.* The consistent theme of the Old and New Testaments is that the Lord desires His people to be blessed with provision and good health (Proverbs 13:23; Romans 8:35–39; Luke

6:21; Revelation 7:14–17; Ecclesiastes 9:11–12; II Corinthians 11:26; I Corinthians 4:11; Luke 9:58; Matthew 6:19–20; 8:8; James 5:16; I Peter 2:19, 24; II Corinthians 12:7–10).

This concept shattered Jessie's already fragile opinion of God. Jesse had secretly believed that God was "a jerk," and these Scriptures seemed to prove the point. Her unwillingness to get involved in missionary outreaches was because of her fear that she would experience worse suffering than any of the disciples had experienced. After all, if God would let little children suffer as Jessie had suffered, what hope was there for her as an adult? When told that those suffering "in Jesus' name" were NOT children, but adults who were very close to God and spiritually protected, Jessie felt a little relieved, but not much. (Core beliefs do not change easily!) Jessie still struggled to understand her parents' culpability in the deprivation she had suffered.

3. *God has ordained that parents, in obedience to Him, provide for their children until they are old enough to seek God themselves.* Infants and young children are not able to cry out to God and are dependent on their parents to provide their basic needs. (I Timothy 5:8; II Corinthians 12:14; Proverbs 31:15; Psalm 128:1–4; Proverbs 14:1; Proverbs 12:11; Genesis 6:21; Exodus 21:9–10; Leviticus 22:13; Proverbs 28:19; Isaiah 58:7–8; Titus 3:14).

When Jessie was able to recognize that her parents had been fully responsible for providing her needs but had not done so, her anger at them increased for a time. She began to see that as an adult, she was more equipped to trust God for the things she needed. As a vulnerable child, she had needed her parents to take care of her, but they had both failed to. A glimmer of hope sparked in Jessie's heart as she realized that it was her parents, not God, who had failed her. She was now responsible for walking closely to the Lord so that she would not make the same mistakes with her children.

4. *God can and will withhold basic necessities from adults*

as a form of judgment for disobedience, unbelief, un-thankfulness, and rebellion. Generally, however, provision is reinstated when His people turn back to Him (Job 20:18, 27–29; Job 29:2–6; Lamentations 1:11,4:9–10; Ezekiel 4:16–17, 12:18–20; Joel 1:14–18; Proverbs 13:25; Deuteronomy 28:47–48).

Ouch! Jessie did not like this point. I almost lost the ground we had gained by listing this as a reason provision is occasionally withheld. This area can be difficult for wounded people to accept because such people already struggle with a concept of God as a mean old ogre. God is compassionate toward those who have been reared in abusive or neglectful homes. He fully understands why they suffer, and He cares about their struggles. It is important to remember that Scripture was written to adults who knew God, not to little children. The intent of God's removing or withholding provision or blessing was always just and was directed at restoring a proper relationship with Him.

Jessie's poverty as a child was an unfortunate consequence of her parents' rebellion and selfishness, not hers. This, too, was a difficult concept for Jessie to grasp. Since her father had failed to care for her and her mother had refused to, except minimally, why hadn't God helped her? Scripture tells us that children do suffer as a result of their parents' sins. They suffer because the consequences of their parents' actions affect them directly. Likewise, they suffer because they have not been taught to see God as a loving, benevolent Provider who wants to take care of their needs.

5. *God promises to take care of the weak and needy if they cry out to Him in the absence of a father or husband.* Sometimes intervention takes place during crisis, but His provision may refer to an eternal solution.

(Psalms 145:14–16, 146:7; Deuteronomy 10:17–18; Exodus 23:10–11; Psalms 107:9; Proverbs 10:3; Psalm 34:6; Isaiah 14:30; James 2:5; Philippians 4:19; Psalm 69:33; Psalm 72:12–13).

Even in the worst child abuse cases imaginable, God has

found ways to hold onto these victims until He can heal the damage done to them. I believe many people suffer for lack of prayers going up on their behalf. We all suffer as a result of living in a fallen world, and there are no true guarantees that we will escape trauma here. At times, God's solution is to take the impoverished child to heaven, which ultimately is His greatest act of care and safety. The fact remains, though, that Jessie's suffering—and that of every child who has ever lived—will be atoned for one day. (We'll discuss God's plan for repayment of evil in chapter 8.)

6. *God's hand of provision often comes through His people.* Believers are exhorted throughout Scripture to provide for the poor and needy, widows, orphans, and even their enemies (Proverbs 22:9, 25:21–22; Isaiah 58:7–8; James 2:14–17; Acts 2:45; Romans 12:13; Ephesians 4:28; I Timothy 5:3–5; I John 3:17; Proverbs 14:21,31; Matthew 6:2–4; Titus 3:14; Proverbs 11:26).

    ❧   ❧   ❧   ❧   ❧

The prosperity doctrine that many embraced in the 1980s seems to have produced a generation of spiritually bankrupt believers who equate God's goodness with physical wealth and the absence of struggle.

    ❧   ❧   ❧   ❧   ❧

One reason Jessie had suffered as much as she had was that her family was isolated. If her mother had been a member of a Christian church, Jessie's deprivation no doubt would have been less intense. Unfortunately, one consequence of her parents' lack of relationship with the Lord was a lack of friendship with others who could—or would—have helped. Jessie's mother's limited social involvements were with others who struggled as much as she did. The only kindness Jessie had ever personally experienced was from the woman who lived down the hall who was not a Christian.

The physical assistance Jessie had received from welfare had been negative and had left her with feelings of helplessness and anger. Eventually, Jessie understood that the core beliefs she held regarding the Lord were based not on His acts against her but rather on her parents' actions. This somewhat novel idea further encouraged Jessie to rethink the reasons for her bitterness. Far from promising a rosy life on earth, Scripture repeatedly warns that suffering and hardships are realities we must contend with (II Corinthians 1:3–11; Philippians 1:29; Romans 5:3; II Timothy 1:7–12).

Even though many people are the recipients of far more than their basic needs, it should not be assumed that experiencing increased prosperity is an indication of blessing. Nor should it be assumed that living in poverty (or in modest circumstances) is necessarily the result of God's displeasure.

In the context of relationship with the Almighty, maturing in the faith is learning to be content regardless of one's circumstances (Philippians 4:11–12; I Timothy 6:8; Hebrews 13:5). Faith in Christ allows the obedient servants of the Lord to experience a consistent state of joy and thankfulness, not only for present provision but also for the eternal hope that awaits them (Titus 1:1–2; Colossians 1:9–4).

Being thankful for what the Lord has given is a biblical theme that carries with it the unyielding message that ingratitude is linked to arrogance and unbelief (Romans 1:18–21; II Timothy 3:1–5; Romans 11:20–22). The flipside of dependence is independence. If we say that we need God to meet our needs, we are really saying that we are dependent on Him, and we should therefore be thankful for His generous gifts. We also recognize that we have a responsibility to use the talents and abilities God has given us to work diligently for Him. Conversely, if our perception is that we have worked hard and earned all that we have, and that it was through our own initiative that we have prospered, it wouldn't make sense to thank God. But, in Deuteronomy 8:10–14, God reminds us not to forget Him and to be grateful for all He has given us.

The Lord's response to this dilemma is clear:

"You may say to yourself, 'I am rich
because of my own strength and power.'
But remember the Lord your God!
It is he who gives you the power to become rich"
Deuteronomy 8:17–18

Being thankful is a heartfelt expression that readily acknowledges that God is, in fact, the Creator and Sustainer of the universe (Hebrews 1:1–3). All provision is seen as a good gift from His hand, brought by His doing (James 1:16–17).

The prosperity doctrine that many embraced in the 1980s seems to have produced a generation of spiritually bankrupt believers who equate God's goodness with physical wealth and the absence of struggle. Focusing on material things as the indicator of true success, we have miserably missed the mark.

It is not in having much or in experiencing hardship that we find the peace and hope that make life worth living. Rather, it is in knowing Christ and the power of His resurrection. We are commanded to set our hearts and minds on things above, which have eternal consequences (Colossians 3:1–4).

Is it wrong to ask for abundance? Should we assume that true spirituality means we must take a vow of poverty and desire nothing of life? Since God's love and commitment to us have nothing to do with the *amount* of physical blessing He pours out, our choosing to deprive ourselves to prove a point to Him is irrelevant. What counts is our obedience to the path God calls us to (James 1:9–10,25; 2:5–6).

❦ ❦ ❦ ❦ ❦

Dependency on God allows us to hold onto
Him in times of poverty and neediness,
knowing that He will provide for us
as we cry out to Him.

❦ ❦ ❦ ❦ ❦

An intimate relationship with the Creator of life places minimal value on the physical and absolute emphasis on the eternal. It also recognizes, however, that it is the Lord who molded the beauty and blessings we enjoy. He created them for us, and He delights in our joyful responses of praise (Proverbs 30:7–9, Matthew 6:19–21,33).

The ability to experience the passions of life and the longings for intimate engagement with all that is good come from Him. For the child of God who knows the wonder of abandonment to His will, life's countless blessings can be richly experienced in poverty. For it is in longing for the intangible that we more fully experience all that surrounds us (James 1:9–11). Conversely, focusing on that which can be seen dulls spiritual awareness to the true beauty reserved for God's dependent children (Philippians 4:4–13; Hebrews 13:5).

We are told to ask of God, for He loves to generously pour out His goodness to all (James 1:2–8). It is foreign to His character and His ways to deprive His children when they come to Him with an open heart. Failure to ask for His provisions and then believe He will respond is equated with being double-minded.

All children daily ask for things from their parents. It would be strange, indeed, to visit a home where small children ask for nothing. Sometimes children's requests are urgent and necessary, but more often the stated desires are associated with longings. In homes where the parents or caretakers are loving, these desires are welcomed and regularly responded to (Matthew 7:7–11).

Tragically, Jessie and her sisters learned early in life that asking for things, needed or not, would only result in her parents' anger or indifference. They learned to rely on their own fragile skills and abilities to survive. Consequently, the core belief that Jessie learned was that it's useless to depend on parents for anything important or necessary. Daddies don't provide, and Mommies make you pay for any expressed need.

Jessie grew up with an internal refusal to trust God with important things because of a generalized belief that He was just like her parents. The rules Jessie lived by were that you have to take care of yourself and do whatever it takes to get what you can. These core values impacted every area of Jessie's life. To break free from the emotional chains that choked her, Jessie had to first realize that she had learned many lies and distortions. Only then was she poised to accept the truth of Scripture.

To change, Jessie had to learn that true dependency on God would result in a confidence that His love and presence are of higher value than the measure of His provision. Change meant that Jessie would joyfully accept an eternal state of dependency in which she would be cared for by the most benevolent Person in the universe. This would allow her to cling to Him in expectation, both for the good gifts He would offer now and for the eternal treasures He has prepared.

Change would allow Jessie to confidently assert a belief in God's ability to provide for her as He chooses and a humble acceptance if His choice of provision was minimal. Since God is always fair and just in His personal dealings with us (Psalm 101:1; Deuteronomy 32:4), Jessie could assume that His actions toward her would always be in her best interest.

Dependency on God allows us to hold onto Him in times of poverty and neediness, knowing that He will provide for us as we cry out to Him (Psalm 68:10; 111:5; I Timothy 6:17). God loves to respond to our needs when our hearts are open and expectant. The self–interest and greediness of a spoiled or demanding child robs any loving parent of any delight in giving (II Timothy 3:2–5). We all know this kind of child. Such children are usually miniature reflections of their parents in character and ways. The truly grateful soul longs to give praise and adoration for all God's bountiful gifts (Psalm 68:10). Its heart ponders His kindness and marvels at His intimate con-cern over its welfare (Psalm 103:5).

Dependent but hard working, expectant and yet content, we journey through life playing out the heavenly contradiction of our reality as believers. Like the writer of Proverbs, we echo the prayer that God would make us neither rich nor poor, for in having too much, we might reject Him and say we don't know the Lord; if we are poor, we might steal and would disgrace the name of our God (Proverbs 30:7–9).

Dependency is an attitude borne out of anticipation and faith. It refuses to believe that God is not related to us and does not care about us. To the contrary, this blissful state looks to the Creator with a wide–eyed confidence that Abba, our heavenly Daddy God, recognizes His responsibility to care for what He has created and does so perfectly when we cease our useless efforts to care for ourselves independent of Him.

Common Problems Of Unmet Physical Needs

Now that we have examined God's design for physical provision, let's look at some of the problems that people who have not had these basic needs met in childhood struggle with. You may not have been able to identify with the severity of Jessie's story but may recognize some of the other symptoms as problematic in your life. Keep in mind that these indicators can also be caused by other factors or a combination of problems. Understanding childhood abuse is not a perfect science, and people respond differently to trauma and deprivation.

Children who have not experienced consistent adequate provision in the areas of housing, food/water, clothing, and health care often struggle with some of the following symptoms. Check any that apply to you.

1. **Housing** –Instability can lead to

Frequent moving . . . . ❑
Rigidity (refusal to move, even when necessary) ❑
Fear of losing home or being forced to move . . . ❑
Tendency to live above means, resulting in
financial problems . . . . ❑
Lack of responsibility in caring for home . . . . . ❑
Rigid requirements that everything
be in its proper place . . . . ❑
Inability to settle down . . . . ❑

Frequent discontent over living situation, including
relationships . . . . ❑
Inability to develop long–term relationships . . . ❑
Lack of meaningful relationships due to
frequent moving . . . . ❑

2. **Food/water**—Insecurity often leads to

Hoarding . . . . ❑
Eating disorders/addictions . . . . ❑
Health problems related to obesity
and poor nutrition . . . . ❑
Emotional dependency problems . . . . ❑
Isolation from relationships . . . . ❑
Inaccurate sense of self–value . . . . ❑
Obsessive–compulsive thinking
and/or behavior . . . . ❑
Preoccupation with physical
looks and weight . . . . ❑
Profound mood swings . . . . ❑
Hiding food . . . . ❑
Comforting self with food . . . . ❑
Lying about food consumed . . . . ❑
Preoccupation with food . . . . ❑
Guilt and shame . . . . ❑

3. **Clothing**—Lack of adequate provision can lead to

Stealing . . . . ❑
Exaggerated focus on looks and attire . . . . . . ❑
Compromised dress ethics due to
peer pressure . . . . ❑
Financial problems related to overspending . . . ❑
Immodest clothing to draw attention to self . . . ❑
Relational problems within family
due to inappropriate focus . . . . ❑
Violence . . . . ❑
Excessively large wardrobe . . . . ❑

Inaccurate sense of personal worth or identity . . ❏
Obsessive concern about being
embarrassed by wardrobe . . . . ❏
Refusal to wear generic or inexpensive labels . . ❏
Need to flaunt wardrobe to friends
and co–workers . . . . ❏
Inappropriate attire or hygiene habits . . . . . . ❏
Refusal to buy necessary or appropriate
clothing . . . . ❏

4. **Health Care** –Lack of provision can lead to

Unnecessary physical ailments in adulthood
that could have been avoided with proper
treatment . . . . ❏
A belief that physical problems are to be
tolerated, not treated . . . . ❏
A tendency to ignore health problems
in your children unless critical . . . . ❏
Hypochondria (obsessive worrying about
own health) . . . . ❏
Financial problems related to hypochondria . . . ❏
A tendency to fake illness to gain attention . . . . ❏

Can you think of other symptoms commonly experienced by those whose physical needs were not met? If you checked more than one box, you may want to talk with a close friend or your pastor or seek out professional help.

Ask your spouse or a close friend whether he/she thinks you have problems in any of these areas. Then, once you are able to identify specific symptoms, ask the Lord to show you how you learned these behaviors and during which ages you were exposed to deprivation or excess in each category. Once you are able to identify core beliefs, the healing process can begin.

Practical Exercises

1. When you were a child, did you feel that your home was a safe place?

2. In what ways did you learn healthy values?

3. Was food overvalued or used as a replacement for comfort?

4. Were your clothing needs met adequately? What was the attitude in your home toward clothing?

5. How did your parents deal with health–care concerns? Did you believe that they cared about your physical problems?

6. Who did you believe was ultimately responsible to take care of your physical needs as a child?

Chapter 7

Protection Needs

A Question of Safety

Lord, your love reaches to the heavens.
Your loyalty goes to the skies.
Your goodness is as high as the mountains.
Your justice is as deep as the great ocean.
Lord, you protect both men and animals.
God, your love is so precious!
You protect people as a bird protects
her young under her wings.
Psalm 36:5–7

*T*his chapter is about protection and safety needs in childhood. This is a particularly relevant area, since many victims point to the lack of safety in their homes as the major reason they turn from God and fear relational intimacy. To convince survivors of childhood abuse and neglect that dependency on the Lord is a good thing, the distortions and pain of betrayal, abandonment, and rejection must be addressed. Additionally, we must not fail to understand how extensive and far–reaching the impact of abuse is in every aspect of a child's developing personality.

This chapter takes a brief look at three particular types of abuse. Chapter 8 focuses on the role each type of abuse plays in destroying a child's natural bent toward dependency. To embrace God's desire and command that we trust in Him, we will have to remove the various emotional barriers that keep us from doing so. In the end, we will see that it is, in fact, the result of abuse and/or neglect that we continue to resist trusting anyone—especially the Lord—with our hearts, lives, and direction.

The three types of abuse we will examine are physical, emotional, and sexual abuse. Since volumes of excellent literature are available on each of these topics, my intention is merely to provide a point of reference that will help determine whether or not you have suffered from any of these forms of abuse.

❧   ❧   ❧   ❧   ❧

It is believed that roughly five children die each day as the direct result of physical abuse.

❧   ❧   ❧   ❧   ❧

If you experience emotional anxiety as you read on but can't connect any memories to your discomfort, that's okay. Many adults who were abused as children learned to repress the memories and feelings that were so painful. Helpful solutions will be offered in the last chapter to pinpoint the reasons for your anxiety.

Some estimates suggest that between 5 percent and 20 percent of all children grow up in healthy families, where love, nurturing, guidance, and safety are provided. If this statistic is correct, that means that 80 percent to 95 percent of us have grown up in dysfunctional homes, where these needs have not been adequately met.

It is believed that roughly five children die each day as the direct result of physical abuse. This figure is no doubt low, because death related to secondary complications may never be reported accurately. In addition, the American Humane Association reported that 1.9 million cases of child abuse and neglect were reported in 1985, but it was certain that the true picture was much worse. Most researchers agree that it is virtually impossible to know the actual figures of childhood physical or sexual abuse, because most incidents are not reported.

In the area of emotional abuse, our tendency is to throw up our academic hands and give up trying to determine the extent of the problem. First of all, professional experts can't agree on a definition of what constitutes abuse or neglect in any of the three areas. Internationally, there seems to be such a variety of standards that it appears impossible to establish a criterion that all clinicians and political structures will accept.

The second problem has to do with the hesitancy to report. Without laws or standards by which to evaluate complaints, there are few who are willing to enter into the judicial system with only the word of a child or a concerned advocate. Even where there have been witnesses to emotional abuse, the laws simply do not address unverifiable incidents.

A third reason any form of abuse is difficult to evaluate in terms of prevalence is the long–standing debate over the privacy rights of citizens. The state is reluctant to interfere with parental authority, especially when the definitions of child maltreatment are so vague. Put more simply, historical and judicial bias has held that the state should stay out of the affairs of the family.

Establishing accurate definitions of the various forms of abuse is difficult and controversial. We will therefore avoid extreme positions that either disregard abuse altogether or include virtually every forceful behavior on a parent's part as abusive.

Definitions Of Abuse

Generally, the National Committee for the Prevention of Child Abuse defines abuse as "an injury or pattern of injuries to a child that is nonaccidental."

Physical Abuse

Physical Abuse is any nonaccidental physical injury that results in welts, bruises, scars, broken bones, or serious internal or pathological injury. Physical abuse that causes brain damage is included in this definition.

In his excellent book *Adult Children of Abusive Parents*, Steven Farmer writes:

> If you were physically abused, you came to associate touch with pain. You learned to associate feelings with hurt and and to be constantly vigilant for the open hand or the switch. The very people you turned to for love and protection became your tormentors. You could find no safety with your parents.

Sexual Abuse

Dan Allender, in *The Wounded Heart*, makes it clear that our definition of sexual abuse is critical. We tend to minimize our own victimization but are quickly appalled if we hear that someone else has suffered the same offense as we did. Dr. Allender offers this definition:

> Sexual abuse is any contact or interaction (visual, verbal, or psychological) between a child/adolescent and an adult when the

child/adolescent is being used for the sexual stimulation of the perpetrator or any other person.

In addition to offering the preceding broad parameters, Dr. Allender expands his view by saying:

Sexual abuse may be committed by a person under the age of eighteen when that person is either significantly older than the victim or when the perpetrator is in a position of power or control over the victimized child/adolescent.

Sexual abuse, whether physical or emotional, is quite possibly the most damaging to a child's soul, leaving the victim in an inescapable prison of pain. Unable to sever the inappropriate bonding that occurs with sexual violation, the child's perception of self and all others is horribly damaged.

❦   ❦   ❦   ❦   ❦

Sexual abuse, whether physical or emotional, is quite possibly the most damaging to a child's soul, leaving the victim in an inescapable prison of pain.

❦   ❦   ❦   ❦   ❦

Sexual abuse victims seem to have a perception of self–badness that far exceeds that of victims of other kinds of abuse. In therapy, we have found that all of our physically sexually abused clients suffered personality splitting, while others who had endured various levels of emotional or physical abuse had generally been able to cope with the violations and survive, emotions intact.

Emotional Abuse

Emotional abuse exists when a child is subjected to demands put on him/her that are beyond his/her capabilities. Teasing, belittling, yelling, and cursing at the child, along with any verbal attacks, would qualify under this definition. In addition requiring a child to emotionally fulfill the role of an absent or negligent spouse falls under this category.

Emotional abuse is the common thread that links all forms of abuse. It is always present and can penetrate the deepest levels of a child's psyche. During formative development, people are most vulnerable to scarring that results from a "sticks and stones" mentality. The careless words and whispers of others traumatize the fragile spirit of our children.

Consequences of Child Abuse

Children who are abused often get offtrack emotionally. They literally stop taking in new information at a heart level and continue to live their lives as if the values they accepted as a child were true. Many adult victims have been frustrated by their inability to emotionally accept the truth they have since learned. As if a time machine had suddenly failed at the moment of abuse, they are able to vividly recall twenty and thirty years later the feelings of despair and self–hatred. With eyes lowered, they often confess having the same self–contempt now.

One client set up a dinner date with her father to discuss his failure to provide the emotional love and nurturing she needed from him. Apart from providing a house and physical necessities, her father had been unavailable to her. For years, she had fought feelings of guilt as she tried to let go of her anger and frustration. Finally, after months of praying, crying, and grieving, she met with her father to discuss her feelings.

The situation was challenging because she was not able to show her father a physical scar that would convince him of the pain he had caused by his neglect. The absence of obvious abuse had allowed her father to deny his failure and to support his position that she had received a better home life than she had actually experienced. Ultimately, her father's denial and self–

deception, along with an emotional numbness that kept him from sensing her pain, won out in their conversation.

She left the meeting feeling discouraged and full of guilt. Old, familiar emotions surfaced like a whip, with which she promptly began to beat herself for her ingratitude. In this case, reconciliation was not possible, because her father was unwilling to extend understanding to his wounded daughter and because his defensive reaction widened the gulf between them.

It is not easy to be a parent who feels inadequate and unequipped to provide the emotional needs of his or her family. When the parent's point of reference was abuse or neglect, the parent would not have developed the skills to provide healthy bonding and attachment. Consequently, the willingness to extend understanding and compassion to parents in such cases can not only serve as a vehicle for reconciliation but also remind us that we, too, have been the recipients of such mercy from the Lord.

Whether physically, sexually, or emotionally abused, children who have been mistreated grow up believing the lies and living out the distortions they learned in childhood.

Chapter 8

Physical, Emotional, and Sexual Abuse

Sing to the Lord!
Give praise to the Lord!
He rescues the life of the needy
from the hands of the wicked...
Why did I ever come out of the womb,
to see trouble and sorrow and
to end my days in shame?
Jeremiah 20:13,18

*A*lan and Cindy are a young couple who found after fifteen years of marriage that the core beliefs they had each developed in childhood were threatening to destroy their relationship. We will examine Alan's and Cindy's perceptions as they were growing up as well as the adult views the couple presented in therapy.

We must recognize the complexity of dealing with two people with core belief distortions who are trying to relate intimately to each other. This may provide an idea as to why the divorce rate is soaring worldwide and why it is so difficult to resolve marital conflicts. Seldom is it true that only one of the partners has critical distortions. In Cindy and Alan's case, you will see how each triggered the other's anger and unresolved pain like a row of firecrackers. The fuse was lit the day they said, "I do." From then on, it became, "I won't."

Alan positioned himself on the couch, leaning hard against one side, with the palm of his hand rigidly propped against his face. Hugging the other end of the couch was Cindy, who had managed to territorially strew a splattering of personal items all around her. I sat across from the couple, resisting the urge to smile at their efforts to avoid contact, and uncontrollably visualized a steamship comfortably resting between them, as if in dry dock.

To understand the progression of Alan and Cindy's dilemma, let's see how each developed core beliefs and values about what a husband and wife are. Notice the cocoonlike unfolding of child distortions into adult rationalizations.

Alan and Cindy's Story

Alan grew up with a father who was emotionally absent and who could no doubt easily fit the description of a workaholic. Quiet at home and seldom, if ever, providing any instruction, leadership, or emotional nurturing, Alan's father spent his evenings reading the paper, watching television, or working in the garage.

Alan at Age 4

"I wish my Daddy would play with me. I ask and ask. He says he's too tired...too busy. Sometimes, I don't think he wants us. He says he has to work hard to provide for me. My friend Steve has a daddy who plays with him. They play baseball and go to football games and have lots of fun. They go fishing, too. My Daddy says he don't have time to do those things. I keep asking Daddy to play with me. Don't do much good."

When asked about feelings shared with his father, Alan could not recall any emotional interactions between them. The only time he was touched was when he was disciplined with a belt. The noticeable absence of his father at special events in his life had been the norm and was eventually expected. Alan's relentless efforts to gain his father's attention and approval had only succeeded in distancing them further. As if utterly incapable of comprehending a child's emotional need for a daddy, Alan's father had progressively withdrawn into deeper isolation, hoping to avoid the uncomfortable looks of rejection and abandonment that flashed occasionally in his children's eyes. Alan's pain intensified as his efforts to gain his father's attention failed.

Alan at Age 7

"He's mean! He's mean! I don't care anymore. I'm sick of him. He comes home from work and eats, smokes, sleeps! That's it. What do I care? He's stupid anyway. He's no man. He don't do anything men are supposed to. He just beats on kids. Great Daddy! He's like a dead person. Mom says so. Boy, is she right! Who needs him, anyway? He's no good for anything. Just sits around like a lump. I don't care. Don't need him. Don't want him. I'm better off without him."

Behind every detached husband is usually a domineering wife who controls the ebb and flow of all family functions. Such was the case in Alan's home. Alan's mother had been sexually abused as a child by her father and had found comfort in a world of isolation and fantasy. The pain of betrayal had long ago hidden itself behind walls of self-protection. All that had been left was the shell of a woman who had dreams of one day becoming a dancer.

The only dance Alan's mother had learned, however, was the dance of anger and of control. Gliding from one end of the house to the other with apparent ease, she was able to keep all her children in line, especially Alan, who was the most sensitive. Barking rules and threatening reprisal from their father, Alan's mother successfully kept her children on edge, fearful, and tense.

Alan at Age 9

"It's confusing. My dad is a lump, but Mom makes me nervous. She gets upset so easy. The other day, I accidentally rode my bike across one of her plants outside. She came unglued! I blamed it on my brother, and he got it! Mom made him sit in his room till dinner and ranted at Dad about it when he got home. My brother got a lickin'. I feel bad, but no way I was gonna get one. Last time my dad beat me, I had bruises for a week. I'm startin to figure out how to keep Mom on my side. She wants me to listen to stuff about Dad. If I do that, she's nice, for a while...sheesh!"

Alan listened to his mother play the "poor me serenade," which all the children were forced to hear regularly: they should obey her commands, the first time every time, and be thankful for the good home she was providing them. As Alan's mother tap-danced across the hearts of her children, the children cowered under a pirouette of pain inflicted by a myriad of bitter, off-key performances.

Alan at Age 12

"I hate it! Geez! If I hear one more story about how hard she has it, I'm going to vomit! I'm sick of being thankful. What is so great about home? My dad's a withdrawn wart, and my mother is a sniveling rag. I hate it. She's getting weirder and weirder. Not only that, but she's been saying some pretty stupid things lately. The other night, she was on one of her "poor me" recitals. The kids weren't listening very good, so she got really mad and yelled at them. It's scary, ya know? I wasn't sure what to do to avoid Dad's belt, so I kinda acted sympathetic to her. It worked! She made the other kids go to bed, and I got to stay up. But...she said some things that were kinda uncomfortable. I mean, Moms shouldn't tell kids stuff about their sex life, should they? Yuck! I listened, but she got really mad when I made a face. I'll have to get the face right if I have to go through this again."

At times, Alan's mother would laugh at the tears the children shed while waiting for their father to return home. The children knew the beatings would be long and painful. Alan made sure he avoided "the rod" by lying and accusing his brother and sisters of offenses he had actually committed. Later, when the sound of his father's strap connected with the back legs of his siblings, Alan had cringed under the weight of guilt. For a time, his deception had bothered him, but he knew he would do whatever it took to avoid his father's belt and the bruises that followed. It was as if the only emotional energy his father could expend was during his angry tirades of punishment.

Rather than risk disapproval from the one parent he had received a token of affection from, Alan would rush in where other children fear to tread—into his parents' bedroom. There, he had become his mother's "little man," a role he played perfectly. Whenever his father failed to provide the sexual and emotional pleasure that his mother pleaded for (which was often), Alan would be invited into her confidence. After listening to the woes of married life with a dead man, Alan would hear his mother's familiar message that he was the joy of her life, that without him her life would be meaningless...no one was more important than Alan.

Alan at Age 15

"I don't know how much longer I can take this. When I was a kid, I kinda liked my mom holding me and stuff...felt kinda good. Things seemed like they would be okay for a while. But uhh, now, she's wanting stuff that's weird. Makes my skin crawl, but I don't know. I mean, it's my mom! She says I'm gonna make some woman a fine husband, and stuff about betting I'll be a good lover. Sheesh! Are Mom's supposed to talk like that? The other night, she wanted to tuck me in. Give me a break! Whose mother tucks a 15-year-old in bed? Well, get this...she didn't kiss my cheek! Gross! I'm gonna figure a way out of here one way or another. My mind feels kinda confused sometimes. I'm not sure what's what. Know what I mean? I mean, I'm not sure I want to get married or anything. What if I turn out like my dad? What if I am like my mother? It's scary."

To maintain his favored child status, Alan learned early to put up with his mother's stroking his head and kisses that lingered in an awkward way. Just to hear that he was wanted and valued made the demands somehow less humiliating.

Eventually, Alan found himself indifferent to his father's lack of attention toward him and protective of his mother's feelings and needs. In an odd way, he had become a surrogate husband to his mother since he was thirteen, and his mother had rewarded him with the attention normally reserved for a spouse.

Alan at Age 17

"The last several years have been very confusing to me. I hate myself for wanting my mom's attention so much.

She makes me feel funny inside when she touches me, but I want it, too. It's weird. I about punched my dad out the other day for upsetting her. It's not sane, man! Really, he didn't do anything, but I got defensive because Mom was upset. She's always upset. I don't know why I protect her. Shouldn't they protect me? I don't even know anymore. I feel like something is wrong inside. I don't want to be close to anyone anymore. It's like I've been ruined. I look at girls and compare them to my mom...Yuck! But, I can't help the feelings. I'm kinda by myself a lot. God help me, if I turn out like my dad!"

Cindy's parental roles were reversed from Alan's, but basically they had impacted her in the same way. A traveling salesman who was seldom around, Cindy's father had introduced Cindy to a world of alcoholism, pornography, and violence. As an only child, Cindy had slowly perished under the abrasive screams of her father and the quiet, whiny complaints of her browbeaten mother. Without the benefit of siblings to buffer the regular shrapnel of her parents' wars, Cindy would physically hide under her bed until the explosions ceased. Shell-shocked and numb from crying in vain, she had eventually found safety in the recesses of her fantasy world.

Cindy at Age 4

"Stop it! Stop it! Mommy, Daddy, stop fighting! Please, stop it! I scared! I scared! Please, please, please..."

Even as an adult, Cindy had continued to relive the terror of her parents' violent fights in her dreams and through flashbacks. These emotional reviews usually caused her heart to palpitate and her mind to blank out for several minutes after each incident, as if she were reliving the actual events.

Cindy at Age 5

"There is nobody to help me. They keep fighting all the time. Daddy gets drunk and yells at Mommy for somethin she

*did. He say somethin about a man Mommy did somethin'
with. I don't know, but they scare me. I hide under my bed and
cry to Jesus, 'Help me, help me, Jesus! Take me away from
here.' I don't know what will happen. My daddy is mean. He
scares me. He yells at Mommy and she screams at him. She
tells him to not yell, because I'm scared...but she yells. I'm so
confused. Why won't somebody help me? Please, Jesus, help
me!"*

As a child, Cindy could sometimes feel quite uncontrollably the split-off parts of her emotions screaming at her to hide! The residual effect of her childhood trauma was that the wars in her heart replayed over and over again, triggered sometimes by harmless phone calls from her aging father.

Cindy at Age 6

*"Look at them across the room. Their faces are stretched
and ugly like monsters from yelling, but I can't hear them. I sit
under the table and put my head down in my lap. My arms
wrap around my knees, so I can't see them now. I go to my
playroom. There's a big chair, and I rock in it, with my dolly. I
don't hear them anymore, and I sing songs that are sweet and
soft. The walls are white, with pretty pictures of the forest.
Sometimes, I go to ocean when I hide. It's nice there, and the
only sound is the waves crashing. That noise doesn't scare me.
I like it. Everything else goes away. I don't hear them anymore.
They are gone...or am I?"*

Cindy had been raised to be "Daddy's precious girl." Her father had privately confided in his small daughter numerous times about her mother's unfaithfulness and sexual dysfunction. Eventually, Cindy had been convinced that her mother was the enemy, and only her daddy really loved her. In his efforts to possess her, he had taken away anything his daughter loved. Once he took her little puppy and gave it to the neighbors down the street. Little by little, he made sure that Cindy never set her heart on anything except him.

As her father solidified his position in Cindy's heart, he would sadly confess that it was a direct result of her mother's frigidity that he drank so much and had become so unhappy and needy of her attention. Cindy's father kept telling Cindy a series of lies, each deepening Cindy's distrust of her mother and directing her heart toward her father. In time, innocent hugs turned to intimate embraces. Trying to pull free from the arms of a giant man, little Cindy found herself trapped and confused. She was too young to understand what was happening to her. All she could do was cry, "Daddy, stop! Stop!" Though her tears were intense and her sobs panicky, Cindy's father laughed and chided her for being a "Mamma's baby."

Cindy at Age 7

"Daddy, why are you doing this? Stop it, please! I want you to let me go! Please, Daddy. Don't do this to me...What are you doing? Daddy, please, stop it... Daddy...please!"

Seven-year-old Cindy had been fighting off her father for three years, only to repeatedly experience a feeling of helplessness that destroyed her fragile resistance. Forced to participate in sexual activity, the little girl was made to pose naked in front of her father's camera. Often, after he had been indulging in alcohol and child pornography, Cindy's father would yell at her to come downstairs and lie on top of him. Petrified with fear that he would beat her if she refused, the frightened child would frantically try to think of a way to escape. She finally found one.

"My daddy yelled at me to come downstairs. I don't want to, but if he comes here, he might beat me. What do I do? Mommy, where are you? Why don't you help me? You're just a frigid, stupid Mommy! I hate you. Help me, Mommy! Daddy's coming up the stairs. He's yelling at me. I have to get up now, or he'll beat me. Jesus, help me go away. Take me to

heaven, please, Jesus. I want to be a good girl. I'll do anything you say, Jesus. Help me, please! But He doesn't help me. Daddy's coming. I have to go now, or he'll hurt me. Close my eyes and pretend. That's what I can do. I close my eyes and think about my secret room. My friend is there. We're safe. Nobody can hurt me. I can see my forest. It's safe...safe. I can't feel Daddy. I can't see Daddy. I can't see anything...I'm gone."

Lost in a world of adults and confusion, there were no safe places for her to turn to. Cindy didn't think her mother would ever believe the things her father was doing to her. She had already learned that Mommy was the enemy and wouldn't care about her plight. Unfortunately, her mother had also learned to survive long ago by shutting down feelings to escape reality. In a perpetual state of emotional numbness, Cindy's mother could neither see nor feel her child's pain. This was a household of three broken people who raged aloud in violent eruption while hiding in secluded personal worlds of secrecy and despair.

As Cindy grew up, she withdrew from life and found comfort in the make-believe world she had created. In time, her father's sexual overtures became a routine part of their relationship. Cindy did not know that her feelings of discomfort were valid. She had learned to despise her feelings and herself. She literally stopped developing her own personality and began mimicking each dominant person that entered her life.

Cindy at Age 16

"It's hard to think about the future. My friends have all decided what they will do. I can't seem to find my place. Deep down, I don't really have a dream or anything. My life these days consists of drinking, drugging, and school. Interesting combo, hey? Well, it's all there is. I have a boyfriend, but I don't care much about him. My dad says I better be careful, because he just wants some...What a joke! The other day, my dad tried to French kiss me, right in front of my mother! No guy out

there could be as dangerous as my dad. Anyway, this guy I'm seeing doesn't interest me much. Actually, nothing does. I kind of feel like the only time I'm able to feel at all is when I do drugs or am loaded. Then it's all kind of fuzzy. I don't know anymore what I'm supposed to feel or do. Everything seems kind of confused. One thing is really weird: I hate my father, but I keep dating guys who are just like him! They all want to possess me, and they don't want me to care about anything else... Guess that's all I know. Being possessed is safe, isn't it? Or is it? I don't know. Really, I don't care. The way things are going, I doubt I'll live long enough to find out."

After leaving home, Alan had become a Christian and eventually went to college and graduate school. He had struggled maintaining relationships with friends and the Lord. Alan seemed to have an internal resistance to intimacy and found that he often lacked the desire to open up to anyone. Consequently, whenever his girlfriends would want to move toward marriage, he would subconsciously find ways to sabotage the relationship. As if it were ingrained in him, Alan would begin to destroy intimacy by criticizing everything about his girlfriends. Then he would complain about their lack of attention. Eventually they would grow tired of his attitudes and his unwillingness to be vulnerable. In time, Alan concluded that he didn't have the ability to love one person for more than a couple of years.

Alan also seemed to struggle with emotional feelings in his relationship with the Lord. He had learned the rules of his faith but had failed to connect with the heart of it. He found himself critical of those who were emotionally demonstrative and maintained the belief that his intellectual approach to Christianity was more stable and reliable. At times, he would secretly begrudge those who seemed to have heartfelt emotion toward the Lord and try to deny a lingering doubt that God didn't love Him as much.

Cindy, on the other hand, had left high school and entered the hippie world of the sixties. In search of something, but unsure of what, she bounced from one relationship to another, each leaving her more and more empty. At age twenty, she felt old and worn-out. She couldn't find a place to fit in and often experienced deep feelings of loneliness. She believed in the depths of her heart that no one was to be trusted.

Each relationship Cindy entered into ended with her running away. There seemed to be an obstacle that kept her from opening up to anyone. Every time a man tried to get close to her, Cindy would escape, either inside herself or by actually moving to another town. The isolation she had found in childhood to protect her continued to be her constant companion.

Eventually, after a near-death experience from a drug overdose, Cindy came to the Lord through a friend. Although Cindy was convinced that God hated her and that He only used people, she was drawn by the love she had felt from her friend. Willing to give God a try, Cindy left her hippie commune and enrolled in a Bible college, where she learned the rules of the faith. But she was unable to find or embrace a loving God. Concluding that Bible college was safer than the streets, Cindy continued her profession of faith and spent the next ten years aimlessly obeying authoritarian leaders who claimed to know God's plan for her life.

Twenty-five years later, Alan and Cindy had collided into each other's walls of wounding and distorted core beliefs. After fifteen years of marriage, both were ready to hang up the gloves and retreat to their respective hiding places. Both had accepted the rules of their faith without believing there was anything else to experience. But middleage had brought unexpected trials neither could understand or cope with.

The peaceful coexistence Alan and Cindy had experienced was based on several principles they had each learned from their family of origin. Alan did not attempt to draw out his wife's emotions but expected that she would open up to him on demand. Along with taking care of the house, the children, and the meals, Cindy was expected to satisfy Alan's every need.

There were unspoken rules about who was in charge. As long as Cindy allowed Alan to lead, the rumblings of war were minimized. This, of course, was a role perversely comfortable to Cindy, who had known only controlling men in her life.

Cindy had found some meaning in her position as a mother. Unable to emotionally bond with Alan, she had found a safe harbor with her children (whom she could control). Even as Alan grew to resent her closeness to their offspring, he made no efforts to endear himself to her.

After the first year of marriage, Cindy had learned to tolerate her sexual relationship with Alan, escaping into her "secret room" whenever he made advances toward her. Alan complained that Cindy was cold and lifeless, although he also refused to be drawn into the dance of intimacy. He complained about their physical relationship and bitterly blamed their problems on Cindy's inadequacies.

Cindy alleged that Alan was often manipulative and controlled her with guilt and constant expectations. Her underlying belief was that he disliked women and was happy only if she was catering to his mood swings and sexual appetite. His frequent anger outbursts and occasional drinking binges had caused any closeness she had initially felt to dissipate.

Alan's reaction to Cindy's criticism was to point out that he would not be so demanding if she were less distant and more attentive to his needs. Alan recalled several incidents when he had attempted to spend quality time with Cindy, only to be met with superficial reasons why she couldn't do it. Alan felt that his wife was unwilling to be vulnerable with him and preferred to be alone with the children or to do things that didn't allow for much conversation.

Alan pointed out to Cindy that he would like to spend more time talking through problems, but they seemed to always get into a fight. Cindy's response was that Alan was interested in talking through problems only if he did all the talking and she listened obediently. Cindy wasn't sure why she reacted so vehemently to his control tactics now, but she expressed the belief that she sometimes felt trapped by his anger and emotional threats. She felt that the children were better company and more interested in accepting her as a person.

The bantering went on until, almost simultaneously, they stopped and looked at each other with curiosity etched on their faces. At once, they realized that they had each married a spouse like their father. Moreover, both were imitating their own mothers in the roles they played out with each other. The thought was at once repulsive and intriguing to both Cindy and Alan.

As the sessions continued, we talked about the different ways Alan and Cindy had been the victims of physical, emotional, and sexual abuse. Damage perpetrated almost four decades earlier had led them both into a tumultuous relationship, full of painful reminders of the past.

Let's take a look at the core beliefs Alan and Cindy had developed as children in the areas of physical, sexual, and emotional protection and safety. See if you can relate to any of the distortions they formed and lived out as adults.

Little Cindy's Core Beliefs About Physical, Sexual, And Emotional Protection

"I don't know what it means to be safe. I don't think it's for me. My Daddy used to beat me all the time with his belt. He'd say, 'I'll give you something to cry about,' when I was scared and sad. He yelled at me when I didn't give him what he wanted. People aren't safe. Sometimes they act like they love you. They touch your head nice and stroke it. Then they want bad things. I don't like to be touched anymore. Mommy is gone inside, like me. I have to take care of her because my daddy is so mean. She cries all the time and says she needs me to help her. I don't feel very safe at all. I don't know when

Mommy and Daddy will be nice and when they will hurt. I used to like it when Daddy drank. He'd be happy for a while, but then Mommy would get mad and they would fight. I don't think anything is for sure. I always have to be ready to run."

Little Alan's Core Beliefs About Physical, Sexual, And Emotional Safety

"Daddies are busy and don't have time for children. They work hard and have to rest at night. Mommies take care of everything at home and have bad tempers. They get to be in charge of things and make everyone else do what they want. The person who runs things can make other people do bad things that feel funny. You have to obey, but then you get special favors. Daddies are angry a lot and spank children very hard. That's how they get children to obey. If you are afraid of Daddy, you won't do bad things. Daddies don't show feelings except anger and being mad. Mommy cries if she doesn't get what she wants. Sometimes she can be nice, but you have to do things for her. I have to be a big man for Mommy, because my dad doesn't treat her right. When I grow up, I'm going to give my wife lots of sex and attention. Then she'll be happy. Mommy says that's what she wants."

Can you see the specific core beliefs Alan and Cindy learned from their parents? Now let's look at the adult versions they presented, beginning with Cindy.

Adult Cindy's Perceptions About Physical, Sexual, And Emotional Protection And Safety

"I'm safe if I make sure no one around me is unpredictable. That's a little difficult, so I make a point of staying away from most people. Alan is loud, but he's mostly mouth.

> *I told him if he ever touches me or the kids, I'll kill him. He doesn't very often. I do the disciplining. Sexually, I don't enjoy Alan, but then, I don't think I would enjoy anyone. I do my duty, like Scripture says, but it's not my favorite activity. Emotionally, I'm safe because I don't let anyone too close. I'm not the type of person that has to have people in my face. I'm more of an introvert and prefer to be alone or with my children. I have a best friend that I feel emotionally open with. We have problems from time to time because she says I'm too posses-sive. I don't get it. I'm really not like that with Alan, but if my friend branches out a little, I get really upset. As strange as it seems, I struggle feeling that if she loves someone else it means she is rejecting me. How do you figure it? I know in my head that's stupid, but I can't seem to let go of the feeling. Alan thinks I'm ridiculous. Sometimes I think I would be better off to not feel anything at all. Emotions are trouble. I can feel God when I worship, but that's about all. There's something about praying and praising that allows me to go into the place I used to go as a child. I can always visualize Jesus there with me, but then afterwards I don't feel anything again."*

Cindy grew up believing emotions were basically to be avoided. Her immediate association with pain had taught her to guard her heart from being exposed to anyone. Because God has designed us to emotionally connect with Himself and others, Cindy had an internal desire she could not understand that longed to attach to someone.

Cindy had not been able to find emotional intimacy with Alan but was able to relate intimately with her best friend. This is often the case for adult victims. The spouse often reminds them emotionally of the abusive parent who caused them so much pain. It is especially common to find women who are finally able to experience emotional intimacy with women friends. The inherent danger, however, is that such women tend to find themselves in emotionally dependent relationships that are a replay of their dysfunctional childhood.

Now let's look at Alan's adult version of his childhood values.

Adult Alan's Perception Of Physical, Sexual, And Emotional Protection And Safety

"People spend too much time digging around, blaming their parents for their problems. If they would just obey Scripture, their problems would go away. I believe the Bible says I'm in charge. I provide physical needs for my family, and Cindy is supposed to give the emotional stuff. Sex is for adults, and I'm an adult. I think Cindy should be available to me in that area, instead of withholding. I don't think it's right. She's kind of frigid, if you know what I mean. How's a man supposed to feel accepted if his wife won't show him any respect? Even my kids act like it's okay to mouth off to me. Cindy has taught them that. I think they should get the rod sometimes because they are defiant and lazy. My son is turning into a "Mamma's boy." Every time I tell him to do something, he runs to his mommy. I don't think it hurts to spank the kids or send them to their room for a while. Cindy has a fit, like it's going to kill them or something. It's what my mom did, and it worked! I think it's important for kids to learn to be mature and obedient. I've had my kids doing adult stuff for years. They are more responsible than most of my friends' kids. My daughter knows how to make a budget, shop, and balance a checkbook, and she's only ten. Since her mother won't do anything, someone has to. Anyway, it's what I learned."

Alan's ideas of what a husband should be had been distorted by his father's passivity and his mother's aggressiveness. In an effort to avoid being a replica of his dad, Alan had mimicked virtually every aspect of his mother's parenting and relational style. Included in that was a more appropriate—but just as damaging—emotional expectation on his young daughter. Although he didn't sexually molest her, Alan had nevertheless turned his attention to his daughter, in place of his emotionally distant wife.

❦   ❦   ❦   ❦   ❦

The sad reality that both Cindy and Alan faced was that they had repeated their family of origin patterns without even realizing it.

❦   ❦   ❦   ❦   ❦

On the other hand, Cindy passively accepted this arrangement because it comfortably resembled her mother and father's relational style. She learned to ignore the caution flags that should have been signaling a growing problem and continued to live in her own world of denial. What she didn't see, she wouldn't have to face. Wasn't that what her mother had taught her?

The sad reality that both Cindy and Alan faced was that they had repeated their family of origin patterns without even realizing it. Although neither of them had engaged in the obvious behaviors or addictive choices of their parents, the same attitudes had been passed on to yet another generation. In effect, Alan emotionally passed on his mother's dysfunction to his children, and Cindy exhibited symptoms of the helpless victim. Both were caught in a web of confusion, laced with threads of deception. Their long involvement in a rules-oriented version of Christianity only intensified their resentment and emotional isolation.

To break free from their denial, Alan and Cindy had to begin to understand how powerful and irrational the core beliefs they had learned in childhood were and how those beliefs still dictated their feelings and values.

As we continue journey down the road to dependency, we find ourselves at a junction. To the left is *The Road Of Reasons*. To the right is *The Road Of Damage*. Straight ahead is a third road: *Keep Going Straight. Don't Turn To The Left Or Right*.

Many strugglers looking for answers start down The Road of Damage because the symptoms seem so clear. In the process, they generally find that the road takes them on a loop to The Road of Reasons and eventually back to where they started. It looks like this:

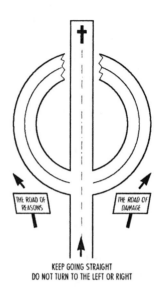

KEEP GOING STRAIGHT
DO NOT TURN TO THE LEFT OR RIGHT

Alan had taken the left turn early in our sessions. He had blamed his passive father and complaining mother for all his problems. His parents had been abusive and neglectful of his needs! Alan felt justified in his efforts to gain genuine love and attention from his spouse.

Cindy initially denied the abuse that simmered beneath her reasons for distancing from Alan. In fact, she wanted to avoid that road altogether. To face her father's sexual abuse and anger was too frightening. She knew that inside was still a terrorized little girl who was torn between wanting to be "Daddy's precious girl" and wanting to kill her father.

Cindy's solution had been to focus on the symptoms and learn a few behavior–modification techniques for dealing with her marriage problems. She was not interested in emotional processing and didn't see any value in digging up the past.

Many of us in our struggle to understand our adult (or not so adult) behavior tend to take either the left road or the right. We give months and years of our attention and resources to dealing with either symptoms or what we perceive to be the roots of our problems. While both approaches are necessary in the overall process, we must be careful not to get off track. Scripture tells us numerous times to avoid turning to the right or the left (Proverbs 4:27; Joshua 1:7; Deuteronomy 28:14; II Kings 22:2).

Knowing that we frequently tend to travel both sides of the road, God promises in Isaiah that "Whether you turn to the right or to the left, your ears will hear a voice behind you saying, 'This is the way; walk in it".'

Let's go to Scripture for a closer look at God's perspective.

Biblical Standard For Physical, Sexual, And Emotional Protection

In virtually every counseling situation where childhood abuse or neglect is confided, the question most commonly asked is, "Where was God when I was being abused?" For instance, Cindy and Alan theoretically agreed for the most part that God was good, just, holy, and loving. On an emotional level, God's "failure" to protect them had resulted in the conclusion that He loved others but not them. This in turn fed their core beliefs about rejection and abandonment.

Even after recognizing that Cindy's father and Alan's mother each had been the abusive parent, Cindy and Alan still struggled emotionally to grasp God's love, to comprehend God's place in their lives. Based on the fact that He had not stopped the abuse, they wanted to know: If God did not love them, as they suspected all along, why should they trust or make any attempt to be dependent on Him? If He protects some but has selective compassion for children being abused and neglected, how could they not despise His inconsistency? Cindy wanted to know what it took to obtain "most favored child" status with the Almighty.

Unable to comprehend His actions and inconsistent demonstrations of benevolent protection, Cindy and Alan had given up believing they could ever trust God with their problems or their lives. Concluding that God's mercy and judgment were unpredictable, Alan and Cindy perceived the Lord in the same way they had perceived their parents. In other words, if

God is unpredictable, He cannot be trusted to act in their best interest.

Dr. Dan Allender provides a compelling answer to the question, "God, where were you?" Frequently quizzed about the Lord's reasons for intervening in some situations and "failing to act" in others, he explained, "When my clients ask me, 'Where was God when I was being abused?' I tell them, He was on a cross, dying." God had already intervened in the only way possible to save those who innocently suffer from depravity.

How could a charge of indifference or favoritism be brought against the Creator of life, who was willing to be insulted, tortured, humiliated, and murdered though He had been innocent? Could the painful cry of confusion and seeming betrayal Jesus felt be so different from our own? Scripture tells us that the chief priests, teachers of the law, and the elders mocked Jesus and hurled insults as they sarcastically questioned God's goodness: "He trusts in God. So let God save him now, if God really wants him. He himself said, 'I am the Son of God'" (Matthew 27:43).

What must Jesus have felt those last moments, after suffering such horrible, undeserved abuse? Having given His entire earthly life to loving His Father's people and pleading with them to return to God, they had responded in rage and violence. Innocent, and no doubt feeling abandoned, He loudly cried out to His Father, "My God, my God, why have you left me alone?" (Matthew 27:43).

Although we cannot be sure what Jesus felt as He uttered those sorrowful words, Psalm 22 paints an image that may help us put His sorrow, and ours, into perspective. As you read the anguished prayer of David, try to open your heart to identify with His suffering. Perhaps you will find that Jesus's final words were recorded centuries earlier for the innocent who have doubted God's concern. Remember that Jesus and King David were deeply loved by God. The fact that God allowed them to suffer cannot be an indication of His disinterest.

Several key points in this portion of Scripture relate to

abuse. But first, it's important to understand the ways this passage *Does Not* relate to children:

1. **The Bible was not written to children**. It was always the major tool godly adults were to use to teach their children about God.

Cindy had not previously understood this point. As a wounded adult reading Scripture, Cindy realized that she was not emotionally mature enough to obey many of the passages and that she had wrongly concluded that she was a "bad Christian." As she began to see that God had intended her parents to teach her His principles of life instead of words and actions of death, Cindy was eventually able to understand why she had not been able to embrace God's word.

In Judaic history, God's deliverance was not tied to either His ability to protect or His desire to do so. The generations prior to King David rightly understood that God's actions were intimately connected to relationship and His sovereign right to unfold His plans as He intended. To them, the world did not revolve around their lives; rather, their relationships and direction were based on God's plan.

2. **The writer of Psalm 22 was an adult, not a child**. He had a rich heritage regarding the Lord and had the emotional maturity and experience to know that God was, and is, faithful.

Children experience God through their parents' teachings and lifestyle. Therefore, it should not be assumed that a child, especially one raised by unbelieving parents, should automatically understand God's promises or plan in relation to them.

If you were deeply wounded by abuse in childhood, try to understand that the Lord is not indifferent to your abusive experience. He responded to your cries for help by providing a long-term solution. The fact that you are reading this book proves that He did "save" you from the torment you endured as a child, even though your deliverance may not have come immediately.

Keep in mind that God's judgment will come in full measure and that God has not "forgotten" any of the things that were done to you! If your abuser has not repented and made amends, he or she will face the Righteous Judge one day and pay for every evil act committed against you (Psalms 37; 73).

The following discussion of Psalm 22 is designed to help you gain a biblical perspective of the pain you experienced and understand how it has impacted you.

1. **David voices the belief that God has abandoned an innocent person, and that He is far away.**

Verse 1: *"My God, my God, why have you left me alone? You are too far away to save me. You are too far away to hear my moans."*

Alan's core belief was that his father had abandoned him. This led him to believe that God did, too. Cindy was like David: she had cried out to Jesus for help and did not understand why He had not come to her rescue.

2. **David expresses his frustration that God is not responding, even though the sufferer has been crying out day and night.** This would no doubt create a belief that God does not care, or He would answer.

Verse 2: *"My God, I call to you during the day. But you do not answer. And I call at night. I am not silent."*

Cindy recalled the hundreds of hours she had cried out to God. She's not quite sure when it happened, but eventually she was able to internalize Jesus emotionally. By closing her eyes and visualizing Jesus holding her in His arms, Cindy was able to experience comfort. This led her to conclude that only in detachment could she experience Him.

3. **David acknowledges that God is enthroned and wor-**

thy of praise for His many saving acts toward Israel in the past.

Verses 3-4: *"You sit as the Holy One. The praises of Israel are your throne. Our ancestors trusted you. They trusted you, and you saved them."*

Alan and Cindy both lacked this belief. They could not think about God being enthroned anywhere. If He were so powerful, why didn't He save them?

4. **David acknowledges that God has been faithful to deliver His people before when they cried out to the Lord for help.**

Verse 5: *"They called to you for help. And they were rescued. They trusted you. And they were not disappointed."*

Again, in this verse, the psalmist is able to recall memories of deliverance he had heard about as a child and had experienced as an adult. Cindy had no such memories. She had not been delivered, in her estimation, until she ran away from home.

5. **Suffering unjustly from his people and facing their ridicule because of his love for God is noted.**

Verses 6-8: *"But I am like a worm instead of a man. Men make fun of me. They look down on me. Everyone who looks at me laughs. They stick out their tongues. They shake their heads. They say, 'Turn to the Lord for help. Maybe he will save you. If he likes you, maybe he will rescue you.'"*

The confusion that comes when one suffers at the hands of those who should be providing love and protection was a problem for both Alan and Cindy. They were aware of suffering unjustly but could not relate to suffering for Jesus. As adults, they had both refused to be in situations where they would have to share their "faith" with a hostile person. Anger was something to be avoided at all costs.

6. **David acknowledges that he has been dependent on God since his birth, and he pleads for God's protection now, since there is no one else to help him.**

Verses 9-11: *"You had my mother give birth to me. You made me trust you while I was just a baby. I have leaned on you since the day I was born. You have been my God since my mother gave birth to me. So don't be far away from me. Now trouble is near, and there is no one to help."*

Being taught as a child that God loves, that God protects, that God is trustworthy, enabled David to believe that deliverance would come again. Alan was certain as a child that his father would not help him. Because of a core belief that daddies don't care about their children's problems, Alan didn't bother to ask for help.

The anxiety of feeling that no one intervened when abuse was happening is a common theme voiced by adult survivors of child abuse. Isolated and unprotected, children become overwhelmed by their circumstances and emotionally detach to survive. Unlike David, they see no other options for deliverance.

Some children have heard of God and cry out to Him but feel that He is ignoring them. Others have been reared in homes where God's name has been uttered only as a curse. Such children have no concept of God as a Deliverer who is able to help them.

7. **David paints a picture of the severity of his situation and continues to plead with God for help.**

Verses 12-14: *"Men have surrounded me like angry bulls. The strong bulls of Bashan are on every side. Like hungry, roaring lions they open their jaws at me. My strength is gone like water poured out onto the ground. All my bones are out of joint. My heart is like wax. It has melted inside me."*

At times, adult victims feel that the abuse they endured was the most horrible offense ever committed. Who can judge? Because no one had helped Cindy, she had eventually concluded that her experience must be "normal." Minimizing the damage is a common element seen in survivors of childhood abuse. As Cindy learned to see her father's abuse as it really was, she was able to cry out and grieve for the atrocity against her soul.

8. **The pain is taking its toll, and David seems to be distancing himself emotionally from his circumstances.**

Verses 15-18: *"My strength has dried up like a piece of a broken pot. My tongue sticks to the top of my mouth. You laid me in the dust of death. Evil men have surrounded me. Like dogs they have trapped me. They have bitten my arms and legs. I can count all my bones. People look and stare at me. They divided my clothes among them, and they threw lots for my clothing."*

These passages struck a cord for both Alan and Cindy. When they realized that their way of escaping the pain of abuse was dissociation, they were able to see that this was a way out that others also used. The thought that God had made it possible to emotionally distance themselves from pain helped both Cindy and Alan to believe that He cared for little children who suffer.

9. **Having been raised to understand his value to God, he is able to regard his life as "precious," even in the midst of the pain, and seems to plead for deliverance based on that fact.**

Verse 20: *"Save me from the sword. Save my precious life from the dogs."*

Alan's core belief was that he held no value for his father and was precious to his mother only if he provided certain favors. The thought that he could be "precious" to God moved him to tears. Cindy, too, had felt unloved and often recalled believing that her life was a mistake. The concept of being valued or special to God was foreign to her. The process of accepting this great truth took months for Cindy and followed only after many tears.

10. **After assuring God of his loyalty, or perhaps after bartering with Him, David declares that God has not "ignored" his suffering, nor has the Lord hidden from him.** In fact, David seems to be pulling himself out of his slump by focusing on God's character, His past dealings with Israel, and the belief that the Lord has listened to his cry for help.

Verse 24: *"The Lord does not ignore the one who is in trouble. He doesn't hide from him. He listens when the one in trouble calls out to him."*

During the healing process, there is a tendency for wounded people to go through a stage where they want to "let it all hang out." For a while, they may quit church, sometimes start cursing, say what they really feel, and basically shred their rules-oriented mentality. Some call it "freedom at last." Others battle a spiritual war inside themselves that can be dangerous.

In spite of great suffering, David never allowed himself to question God's goodness or His character. Regardless of his circumstances, David held firm to the understanding that God was deserving of praise and worship. This was a difficult concept for Cindy. Once she allowed herself to face the pain of sexual abuse, she went through a period where she wanted nothing to do with church, God, or anyone else. She had to make a firm commitment to the Lord, and stick to it, to get through the valley of the shadow of death. Alan, on the other hand, was able to grieve his losses and embrace God almost immediately as the kind of father he had always wanted. He seemed relieved to know that God was not like his father and that finally he (Alan) could view himself as a valued son.

11. **The rest of the passage sketches a picture of worship and adoration even though David's circumstances had not changed at that point.** David is certain that posterity will serve the Lord and that future generations will continue to praise God for His deliverance.

Verse 27-31: *"People everywhere will remember and will turn to the Lord. All the families of the nations will worship him. This is because the Lord is King. He rules the nations. All the powerful people on earth will eat and worship. Everyone will bow down to him. The people in the future will serve him. They will tell that he does what is right. People who are not yet born will hear what God has done."*

Even though David was "emotionally based" and at times impulsive, he was able to gain perspective, first and foremost because he possessed an accurate concept of God's character and ways. Also, David knew that he was a son and therefore highly valued by God, his Father. His strengths included an overall obedience, loyalty, and openheartedness toward the Lord. Simply put, David refused to question the Lord's goodness and instead resigned himself to accept his lot as apportioned by the Lord.

Understanding God's worldview and the eternal strategy He has been unfolding since the beginning of time becomes critical if we are to work through our distortions about our past, our present life, and our future. To comprehend God's plan in any measure, we must be willing to step outside our experience to view a bigger picture. In other words, rather than judge God by our experience, we must judge our experience against God's word!

The following diagrams show the wounded child's perspective, the adult victim before he/she works through his/her abuse, the adult survivor of childhood abuse who is beginning to understand God's heart, and, finally, what might constitute the Lord's worldview or perspective:

Wounded Child's Perspective:

In the child's view, everything centers around the child's life. Children are egocentric and can see only what is before them. They have no way, cognitively or emotionally, to objectively evaluate their circumstances. Likewise, they lack the ability to understand that the violations against them are a reflection of the abuser's problems and not of their "badness." Since children are not able to comprehend circumstances outside their limited world, everything has an incredible impact on them.

Wounded Adult Victim of Childhood Abuse or Neglect Who Has Not Worked Through Distortions:

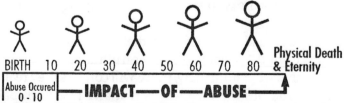

The adult victim of child abuse can recognize that the actual violations occurred a long time ago and lasted for a relatively short period of time. Considering the full span of life, adult victims tend to see their existence as an unpleasant continuation of their unfortunate roots. Without an accurate concept of God or His ways and lacking a commitment to follow, they tend to make major and minor life decisions that reflect their self-value, or lack of it. They frequently select spouses or partners, friends, and employment that reflect their core belief that they "deserve" to suffer. Ultimately, they don't believe that their lives will get any better until they die. Unbelievers tend to view death as a jumping-off point, to escape the misery they had on earth. Sometimes they think death is the end of the road. At other times, they hope that there really is some kind of deity who will take them to a better place once they die. Christians who were taught a distorted concept of God tend to accept their misery in this life and hope for something better in eternity.

The Adult Survivor of Child Abuse, Who is Working Through Their Wounds:

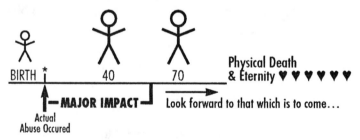

Adult survivors who are able to work through core belief distortions and progressively accept God's point of view will experience tremendous relief from their emotional pain. Not only will they find it easier to accept the truth about themselves, God, and others, but ultimately, peace will come as they realize that God's true destiny for them is rich and free from pain. Rather than live out their lives in woundedness and detachment, adult survivors will begin to focus on eternity and shift their overall attention from self to God. Major and minor choices will begin to reflect a healthier understanding of a worldview that is God-centered rather than self-centered.

By honestly working through core belief distortions, Alan and Cindy were able to develop the ability to put blame where it belonged and to take personal responsibility for the self-defeating choices they had made in their lives. The changes that came almost immediately impacted both of them in a positive way. The quality of their life, family, and budding relationships with the Lord found expression in emotional and intellectual outlets. They began to desire closeness rather than isolation, communication rather than silence. Both developed new interests in learning and expressed levels of creativity they never knew existed. Instead of avoiding the Lord or Scripture, they found that there was an emotional and intellectual desire to understand and experience more of God and Christianity. Alan joined a ministry team that went door to door sharing the gospel. Cindy wasn't interested in that type of evangelism, but was able to share her new faith at a small Bible study with other women. They began to understand that much of the pain suffered since childhood had come, not from the original abuse, but as a result of the self-defense mechanisms they had both generated and exercised as adults.

God's Viewpoint In Relation To Abuse

Each ♥ represents a hundred years

0 - ♥ ♥ ♥ ♥ ♥ ♥ ♥ ♥ ♥ ♥ ♥ ♥ ♥ ♥ ♥ ♥...Judgement Day & Eternity

(The Law)   (Jesus + Cross) = Impact

This diagram does not minimize the sorrow or devastation wreaked on victims of childhood abuse, but rather puts it in perspective. During the course of history, God has implemented various sacrifices to deal with sin and rebellion. The reason such sacrifices have been necessary is man's continual refusal to love and serve the Lord, along with his increasing depravity. Jesus' impact is the critical difference between our worldview and God's. While we tend to focus on our life, our woundedness, etc., the Lord focuses on His strategic plan to usher in the Kingdom of Jesus Christ.

❦ ❦ ❦ ❦ ❦

Impatience is a characteristic of immaturity, not of divine strategy. In other words, since God is actively and sovereignly orchestrating events that will tumble the kingdom of darkness, He need not stop now to set up court.

❦ ❦ ❦ ❦ ❦

Within His kingdom, there will be no hint of self-interest, brokenness, or depravity. We will be free to focus on the worship and adoration of our King. Within His viewfinder, we will see a judgment day where every wrong will be righted, every sin atoned for, and every loving deed rewarded. God will righteously and compassionately recall the events of evil committed against His little ones and will justly condemn the unrepentant. His holy anger will burn against those who destroyed the hearts of children for their own selfish purposes. We will see the dam of tears burst as He replays the sorrow He has felt as well as the pain He has seen and endured. With Him our sadness will begin to wane and the tears will dry, as we finally see justice accomplished.

God does not need to intervene directly in each situation now, for His plan includes a complete recompense in the days to come. His divine will does not guarantee protection during this lifetime. Obviously, living in a fallen world with Satan controlling nations and individuals, He would have to remove us out of the world to protect us. However, in eternity, there will cease to be a question of safety, for the Almighty is even now setting the stage for the final showdown between light and darkness. The result is guaranteed, and it is only a matter of time until God makes His enemies a footstool at His feet (Hebrews 10:13). Impatience is a characteristic of immaturity, not of divine strategy. In other words, since God is actively and sovereignly orchestrating events that will tumble the kingdom of darkness, He need not stop now to set up court.

As you reflect on the following passages from Psalm 10, try to remember that God has not "forgotten" any of the wounds inflicted upon you and that He promises vindication. Read slowly and meditate on the Psalmist's concern. Perhaps you will be able to identify and rest in the conclusion he was able to draw even while the suffering continued:

Lord, why are you so far away?

Why do you hide when there is trouble?

Proudly the wicked chase down those who suffer.

The wicked set traps to catch them.

They brag about the things they want.

They bless the greedy but hate the Lord.

The wicked people are too proud.

They do not look for God.

There is no room for God in their thoughts.

They always succeed.

They are far from keeping your laws.

They make fun of their enemies.

They say to themselves,

"Nothing bad will ever happen to me.

I will never be ruined."

Their mouths are full of curses, lies and threats.

They use their tongues for sin and evil...

They look for innocent people to kill.

They watch in secret for the helpless...
The poor are thrown down and crushed.
They are defeated because the others are stronger.
The wicked think, "God has forgotten us.
He doesn't see what is happening."
Lord, rise up and punish the wicked.
Don't forget those who need help.
Why do wicked people hate God?
They say to themselves, "God won't punish us."
Lord, surely you see these cruel and evil things.
Look at them and do something.
People in trouble look to you for help.
You are the one who helps the orphans.
Break the power of wicked men.
Punish them for the evil they have done.
The Lord is King forever and ever.
Remove from your land
those nations that do not worship you.
Lord, you have heard what the poor people want.
Do what they ask. Listen to them.
Protect the orphans.
Put an end to suffering.
Then they will no longer be afraid of evil people.

The psalmist knew that it was good to cry out to God and to plead for justice. Even when it looked as if the weak and helpless were losing, he knew that evil people would eventually pay for their sins and that God's justice would someday reign. He also knew that God responded to prayer, and so he continued to seek the Lord for relief.

We, too, have the responsibility and privilege of bringing our pain to the Lord, believing that He will respond. Maturing in the Christian faith means that we persist in hating the things that God hates (such as abuse) and fighting to stop them. It also means that we battle the greater problem of evil on our knees in prayer, confident that God will hear, will answer, and will overcome evil in the end.

Common Problems Of Childhood Abuse

If you are able to relate to any of the symptoms on the following list, check the corresponding box. Remember that we all have various degrees of dysfunction. Try to identify those symptoms that jump off the page. Chapter 11 will set a course for working through the areas you checked. Generally, if you marked more than two areas, you may have several problems currently bothering you as a result of childhood abuse.

1. Victims of physical abuse often display some of the following symptoms:

   Inappropriate anger or rage . . . . ❏
   Aggressive or violent behavior . . . . ❏
   Chronic depression . . . . ❏
   Chemical addiction . . . . ❏
   Process Addiction . . . . ❏
   Abusing spouse . . . . ❏
   Abusing children . . . . ❏
   Resistance to authority figures . . . . ❏
   Engaging in pornography . . . . ❏
   Engaging in fantasies of hurting others . . . . . . ❏
   Difficulty developing or maintaining
   intimate relationships . . . . ❏
   Emotional difficulty being vulnerable . . . . . . ❏
   Verbally and emotionally abusive to others . . . ❏
   Tendency to be moody and unpredictable . . . . ❏
   Tendency to be controlling and manipulative . . ❏
   Personality splitting . . . . ❏

2. Victims of sexual abuse often display many of the following symptoms:

Irrational fear . . . . ❑
Eating disorders . . . . ❑
Precocious sexuality . . . . ❑
Loss of personal identity . . . . ❑
Withdrawal . . . . ❑
Distrust . . . . ❑
Self-destructive behavior . . . . ❑
Sexual promiscuity . . . . ❑
Sexual identity confusion . . . . ❑
Passive dependence (the doormat syndrome) . . ❑
The need to control . . . . ❑
Sexual dysfunction . . . . ❑
Suicidal tendencies . . . . ❑
Difficulty developing or maintaining intimacy . ❑
Personality splitting . . . . ❑
Anger control problems . . . . ❑
Chronic depression . . . . ❑
Chemical and/or substance addiction . . . . . . ❑
Pervasive feelings of shame . . . . ❑

3. Victims of emotional abuse that did not also include physical or sexual abuse may display some of the following symptoms:

Feelings of inadequacy . . . . ❑
Poor self-identity . . . . ❑
Feelings of abandonment or rejection . . . . . . ❑
Chronic depression . . . . ❑
Sexual promiscuity . . . . ❑
Anger control problems . . . . ❑
Passive dependency . . . . ❑
Inability to develop or maintin
intimate relationships . . . . ❑
Resistance to Authority Figures . . . . ❑
Passive-aggressive behavior . . . . ❑

Addictive tendencies (especially workaholic) . . ❑
Perfectionism . . . . ❑
Pervasive feelings of shame . . . . ❑
The need to control others . . . . ❑

In the final area of dependency needs, we will examine one of the most important and most neglected areas in child development. As we journey toward greater intimacy with the Lord, we will begin to understand the critical role emotional-nurturing plays in the overall development of a child's personality and relational makeup.

Chapter 9

Emotional Nurturing Needs
A Matter of Bonding

You know that we treated each of you
as a father treats his own children.
We strengthened you, we comforted you,
and we told you to live good lives for God.
It is God who calls you to His glorious kingdom.
I Thessalonians 2:11–12

*M*any areas that affect the child's core beliefs about life, relationships, and God, such as the extending of compassion, freedom, forgiveness, empathy, and eventually separation, are necessary for healthy development.

In this final area of need, we want to set the stage for a lost and misunderstood concept. Until about the mid–1970s, emotional–nurturing was an aspect of parenting largely dismissed by both the academic and the Christian community. Most of us grew up in an era where the ability to provide physical needs was the measure of success in parenting.

Following the depression of the 1920s and 1930s, providing for a family's basic necessities generally meant that Mom and Dad had to work long hours.

After World War II, the trend that had started out of need to survive progressively turned into a norm. With reduced financial pressure and a new taste for what two incomes could mean to a family's perceived quality of life, children began to experience less maternal nurturing and more daycare madness. In the late 1950s and early 1960s, the controversy heightened as women began to assert themselves in new ways.

Ultimately, the greatest loss has been in the area of relationships. People no longer have time, energy, or heart to experience and share in the joy of emotional intimacy. Many have become masters of task and losers at love. People have long ago lost the ability to love one another deeply from the heart, if, in fact, they ever had it.

So, what is the problem? We have all read enough books to be experts by now. We have memorized every Scripture on family and have attended numerous workshops and institutes. Yet, we still grapple with failure and confusion. Even in Christian homes where parents attempt to practice a biblical standard and are knowledgeable of the concepts, application is difficult. Why is that?

In theory, the problem is that you can't pass on what you have not experienced. It is the equivalent of a car mechanic trying to operate a spaceship! Years of training are required in addition to practice and more practice in specific tasks before an astronaut can fly to the moon.

To understand the significance of emotional–nurturing needs, we will examine the following aspects of this category: (1) bonding/attachment, (2) belonging/significance, (3) love/acceptance, and (4)self–concept/identity.

Bonding/Attachment

The first crisis that we face in life—as the umbilical cord is severed and the first independent breaths are drawn—is a state of isolation. For a brief moment, the terror of being disconnected causes the new infant to cry out in panic. After a brief interlude, the small bundle is placed in the mother's arms to be comforted and bonded.

The Bible has wonderful illustrations that compare our Abba Father's care for us with that of a nursing babe. "This is what the Lord says: 'I will give her peace that will flow to her like a river...Like babies you will be nursed and held in my arms. You will be bounced on my knees. I will comfort you as a mother comforts her child" (Isaiah 66:12–13).

❦   ❦   ❦   ❦   ❦

Without consistent and repeated nurturing
experiences, especially during the first
two years of life, babies do not develop
the ability to bond or attach easily.

❦   ❦   ❦   ❦   ❦

For the infant, attachment is a means of experiencing comfort and safety at the mother's breast. It is the essential bond that conveys the goodness of dependency and the rightness of belonging. Literally, to attach is to be connected to someone or something else. God has designed life that way.

During the first two years, babies are designed to learn that even in their desperate neediness, they can trust, their world is relatively safe, and their environment is predictable. In an unconscious effort to internalize their feelings, the infant and toddler provide thousands of opportunities for their caregivers to be there for them in their time of need.

If successful and healthy, the baby internalizes the mother along with the nurturing experiences he/she has had. As time goes on, the fragile young child endeavors to develop emotional object constancy. The ability to feel safe, even when alone, to trust that the nurturer will return to meet his/her needs again.

During this critical time of development, the child must experience consistent emotional–nurturing and adequate provision of safety in his/her environment. Harm to the infant results in the infant's withdrawal and isolation. Connecting becomes more difficult and can threaten the child's ability to mature in this essential characteristic of early development. Thus, the mother's role is critical in providing comfort, gentleness, and safety for her baby along with the baby's basic needs. In his letter to the Christians at Thessalonica, Paul wrote, "But we were very gentle with you. We were like a mother caring for her little children" (I Thessalonians 2:7).

It is also during this first stage of life that babies begin to collect a sense of who they are. In other words, as they respond to the kind words and gestures of their primary caregivers, infants display the first signs of personhood and belonging.

In our fast–paced world, where mothers hurry back to work shortly after delivering their babies, it's no wonder that an emotional deficit reaches deep into the child's soul. Without consistent and repeated nurturing experiences, especially during the first two years of life, babies do not develop the ability to bond or attach easily. If left alone, cold, wet, or hungry for hours, they internalize the experience of isolation and eventually accept it as normal. If this pattern continues throughout their childhood, they will lack the necessary skills to attach or bond to others.

Belonging/Significance

Feeling a sense of belonging and familial significance is critical to a child. Children learn about their value and purpose largely as a direct result of their parents' actions and emotional expressions toward them. Gestures that convey importance and family belonging are critical if the toddler is to feel grounded and stable. Many a tear has been shed by confused and rejected children as they have tried to understand why their mommy and daddy don't want them. We see this principle vividly in Scripture in our relationship to Jesus. "I am the vine, and you are the branches. If a person remains in me and I remain in him, then he produces much fruit. But without me he can do nothing. If anyone does not remain in me, then he is like a branch that is thrown away" (John 15:5–6).

The condition of being isolated from the vine is the equivalent of being disconnected from our mother. Unfortunately for many children who are reared in dysfunctional homes, relational isolation is the norm. Caregivers must make a purposeful effort to develop a sense of belonging and significance. Values and beliefs are taught by parents, shared by each family member, and privately experienced in the form of special family bonds.

If these values are properly demonstrated, there is no favored child, for each child has a unique role within the family system that no other child can fill. One of the greatest harms that can be done to children (who experience their own value through their parents' eyes) is to give them the impression that they are less valuable than one of their siblings. Many children have forfeited their own personality and giftings in an effort to win their parents' approval. How tragic it is when a caregiver conveys to a small child that he/she is not as bright or as cute as a sibling! Careless words do great damage to the fragile heart of a child.

To belong means that one is special just the way he/she is. The child who has handicaps or is less intelligent or attractive than his/her siblings is still wonderfully unique and has a place of significance in the family that no one else can fill. This would, of course, be the ideal, but in truth, few of us grew up with such beliefs about our worth. For many of us, a quick review of familial history would reveal the belief that we were not special and could not gain approval from our parents, even with our best efforts.

Did you enjoy feelings of belonging and significance in your family? If not, perhaps you can draw comfort from God's response to familial isolation and disappointment: "If my father and mother leave me, the Lord will take me in" (Psalm 27:10). King David also knew that God could be counted on to adopt abandoned children when he wrote: "He is a father to orphans. He defends the widows. God gives the lonely a home" (Psalm 67:5–6).

Love/Acceptance

Have you ever stopped to consider what is meant by the many sentiments of love that are freely distributed through various media forms? Soap operas would have us believe that love is a sexual attraction that is energized for short durations. However, when it seems to be losing its heat and passion, the relationship usually ends with one or the other moving on to someone else. Within Christian circles, where there is better information about what love really is, the inability to consistently express it intensifies hiding patterns. Where there is no understanding, there is little expectation. Many of us grew up singing, "Jesus loves me, this I know, for the Bible tells me so." When it came to experiencing love as little ones, we learned distortions to this tune and grew to believe that it, too, was a nice idea, but probably not true.

Little children need the kind of love that wills their highest good and carries a smile with it. Such love is demonstrated in the expression of praise when a child wins and the look of compassion when he/she loses. It carefully attends to the child's needs and looks for other ways to express itself. Love is not skin deep or shallow. Its boundaries exceed kindnesses returned, and it seeks to forgive those who have wounded us. It is impossible to "make," and it must be carefully and tenderly developed. Love happens when the heart and the mind dance together.

A child who is loved will grow up believing he/she can do anything. A child rejected or ignored will struggle to find his/her way in life. Always in the child's mind will be the fleeting fear that if my own parents don't love me, who will? Love makes us live, and it makes us die. It sacrifices itself for the sake of the beloved and doesn't show regret. The child who is raised being told regularly that he/she is a blessing and a joy will go much farther than the child who grows up believing that he/she has been a nuisance. The need to experience and feel love is designed into the heart of a child by God. The kind of parental sentiment that does not hold and hug, soothe and rock, fails the test.

One of the ugliest things Satan has done has been to pervert the very meaning of love. Adults who say "I love you" to small children to gain sexual favors from them have made many healthy parents afraid to touch their own children for fear of being misunderstood! Without consistent demonstrations of "good touching" from parents, children will struggle with core beliefs of abandonment and rejection.

Self–Concept/Identity

I have purposely chosen the word *self–concept* over the more commonly used term *self–esteem* because it conveys a more accurate reflection of Scripture. By definition, self–esteem means "The esteem or good opinion of oneself; vanity." According to Webster's Encyclopedic Unabridged Dictionary, to esteem something is "to regard, consider, think, believe or to set a high value on it." A concept, however, is merely a thought or idea about something, a belief system, if you will.

Psychologists like Abraham Maslow and Carl Rogers have made us begin to see our need for self–love and self–esteem. This whole movement was necessitated by an increase in suicide, murders, divorces, depressive disorders, and general dissatisfaction with life. The reasons repeatedly cited for antisocial behavior or self–destructive actions were poor self–esteem and feelings of worthlessness. Numerous theologians and Christian psychologists have joined in to declare that self–esteem is the number one need for people to find value in life.

In his book, *Christian Child–Rearing and Personality Development*, Dr. Paul Meier writes:

> ...one of the most important things we can do for our children is to develop within them an emotionally healthy and Scripturally accurate self–concept. Without self–worth, our children will not only have a miserable life, but they will also be unable to reach the potential God has called them to reach. I firmly believe that all emotional pain ultimately comes from three root sources: (1) lack of self–worth, (2) lack of intimacy with others, and (3) lack of intimacy with God. A poor self–concept can significantly hamper us in all three of these essential areas.

Having a healthy self–concept (that is, a God–centered concept of ourselves) requires that we see ourselves as we really are. It means that we are thankful for our strengths and use them to serve God and others. We also recognize our weaknesses and endeavor to change them with God's help and with the help of our families and friends. It means that we are free to make choices and are responsible for the choices we make. We blame no one but ourselves when we fail, and we humbly acknowledge praise when we succeed. A God–centered concept of ourselves allows us to respond to truth without fear that the truth will change. It gives us a solid foundation from which to build our spiritual lives. A concept of self based on God's standard lets us rest, for we know that the standard will not change.

When a child's well–being is dictated by outside circumstances, the child suffers from what is called "external locus of control." It is almost impossible for the child to feel stable, and any crisis can alter the child's value or sense of happiness. External locus of control is typically found in adults whose parents failed to give them freedom in decisionmaking. This is especially seen in mother/daughter relationships. The mother picks out the child's clothes, friends, and activities and even tries to control the child's thoughts, feelings, and beliefs.

❧   ❧   ❧   ❧   ❧

Though we may struggle at times to
understand why God loves us, the
consistent, gentle whispers of acceptance
are always there, both in God's guidance
and in the way the Lord provides for us.

❧   ❧   ❧   ❧   ❧

Internal locus of control means that the individual's decisions are primarily dictated by the individual's internal sense of direction. If the person feels or thinks a certain way, that's what counts! This, too, can lead to problems because, as humans, we each have flaws that can make us feel one way today and another way tomorrow. Our happiness then depends on ourselves. This type of control limits its vision to our own understanding and perception. We make decisions based on what we see, feel, and think. It provides more stability than external locus of control but inherently lacks the dimension that only God can add. Adults with internal locus of control often struggle with authority figures, especially those who manipulated them in the past.

Upward locus of control is the process where we derive our value and that of others, based on God's foundation. Since God does not change and perfectly loves and values us, we need not fear instability. God's standard for our worth or self–concept is what we look to. God's word says we should praise Him because He has made us in an "amazing and wonderful way" (Psalm 139:13–14). We are jewels in His kingdom and precious to Him. Upward locus of control allows for internal decision making as well as external influence from others, provided they do not contradict God's absolutes or principles.

Though we may struggle at times to understand why God loves us, the consistent, gentle whispers of acceptance are always there, both in God's guidance and in the way the Lord provides for us. Truly the perfect parent, God does not play favorites and always has time to embrace, comfort, show compassion for, and teach us. He does not allow us to stray too far from Him before discipline sets in, and He welcomes us back with warmth and forgiveness as we respond to His parental reproof.

As replicas of His likeness, parents are to impart a sense of a healthy self–concept to their small children that lets their children relax and feel good about themselves. The children should not be overly praised, for that breeds arrogance; neither, however, should their achievements be ignored, for this causes discouragement and feelings of rejection.

Finding the "perfect" balance of imparting a healthy self–concept is not humanly possible. That's why children are designed to cope with some degree of parental contradiction without horrible consequence. The best chance of offering our children the kind of healthy development they need is tied to our relationship with the Lord.

To break the distortions learned in childhood, we each need to relearn the truth God intended us to experience. As we grow "in the grace and knowledge of our Lord and Savior Jesus Christ" (II Peter 3:18) and our hearts begin to open to Him, some of the losses we sustained in our youth can be worked through and grieved. Chapter 11 will look at the specific ways we can change the core beliefs we have learned about ourselves, God, and others.

Practical Exercise

1. When you think of emotional–nurturing needs, what does your experience bring to mind?

2. If your parents were nurturing, what kinds of things did they say and do?

3. Were you able to feel attached and bonded to your family? If not, what was your experience like?

4. Did your parents consistently demonstrate actions of love toward you? What were they?

5. What did you learn as a child about your self–concept?

6. Did you feel that your family regarded you as a significant member? If not, how did each family member treat you? How did you feel about your family while you were growing up?

7. Does your decisionmaking stem from an external locus of control, internal locus of control, or upward locus of control? Explain your answer.

Chapter 10

Bonding/Attachment, Belonging/Significance, Love/Acceptance, Self–Concept/Identity

Lord, my heart is not proud.
I don't look down on others.
I don't do great things,
and I can't do miracles.
But I am calm and quiet.
I am like a baby with its mother.
I am at peace, like a baby with its mother.
Psalm 131:1–2

*T*aylor came to therapy complaining of depression and severe anxiety. She had found herself in several situations where feelings of helplessness were eroding her ability to handle the pressure or confront her problems. She could not put her finger on the reason she was falling apart and consequently felt a growing emotional need to isolate herself from her husband, friends, and peers. In addition, Taylor felt an old familiar temptation beckoning her toward the refrigerator for a glass of wine to soothe her nerves.

As we evaluated her current dilemma together, several of Taylor's core beliefs regarding emotional needs began to emerge. As you read her story, see if you can pinpoint the underlying roots in her childhood that resulted in feelings of worthlessness and despair.

Taylor's Story

The oldest of two girls, Taylor was the child of two alcoholic parents. From her earliest years, she had learned to respond immediately to her father's "hup to" and her mother's controlling demands. She felt like a puppet whose only purpose in life was to make her daddy look good and her mommy happy. This, of course, was impossible, for her parents' demands and expectations far exceeded her abilities.

Taylor has few memories of life at home as a small child, but she does recall feelings of isolation and loneliness. Her mother insisted that Taylor had been attentive and loving, but Taylor has no such memories. It was as if her mother's version of the story belonged to someone else, not to her. Still, because she had grown to accept whatever Mommy said as true, Taylor was confused about her own self–perception yet she could not accept her mother's perception of her. She did not recall ever being held or stroked. There were no kind words or gentle expressions in Taylor's memory. No one said, "I love you" or "You're special." In fact, from the earliest point, Taylor did not feel important at all and had no idea what it meant to be nurtured.

Taylor at Age 3

> *"Mommy dresses me up like a little doll. I don't like it. My head hurts from the tight rubber band. Daddy tells me to smile nice and say, 'Yes sir,' when his other men are around in uniforms. Daddy looks nice, but he never touches or hugs. He tells me I will get his white clothes dirty if he picks me up. Mommy tells me to not say anything...just smile. I don't know what to smile about. I have to sit on the couch, with my hands folded. I want to go play, but Mommy says, 'No, you'll get dirty!' Is it bad to play and get dirty?"*

Taylor's little sister looked like a princess. She was small and petite and had lovely long hair that draped her shoulders. Their mother usually fixed her sister's hair in a French braid, which Taylor secretly hated. All she ever got was a pony tail that pulled her eyes back into her head and made her feel frumpy. And Taylor was chubby. She didn't know why. Perhaps it was because she wasn't allowed to play enough and burn off the calories. Her little sister was naturally skinny, a fact Taylor hated.

Taylor at Age 6

> *"See how Mommy and Daddy talk about my sister? She is 'so pretty' and 'so smart' and 'so much a lady.' One of my daddy's friend's said I was very nice and polite. My daddy just shrugged and told the man that he keeps me in line. Mommy buys my sister nice, pretty clothes but tells me all the time how expensive it is to get dresses for chubby girls. I don't think I am very pretty. I wish I could be like my sister."*

Although he was gone to sea most of the time, Taylor's father assumed the tutoring job for his daughters when he was home. It was a toss–up which of her parents she hated more when it came to help with schoolwork. Taylor's mother refused to help her unless it was late at night after several drinks. Her father's anger and impatience caused so much internal tension that Taylor would make more mistakes with him than without him. Her sister sailed through school with straight A's and no assistance.

Taylor at Age 9

> *"I'm so stupid! Why can't I do this stupid schoolwork? Daddy makes me so nervous. I make one little mistake and he flies off the handle. He says he wishes he could have made another kid like my sister! I hate her! She doesn't have to study at all. I can't stand it! I need help, but they both make me so nervous. Dad actually suggested that my sister help me with math. I couldn't believe it! I wanted to die!"*

As she approached adolescence, Taylor struggled with many aspects of growing up. She was physically developing in ways that made her uncomfortable, and she didn't understand what to do about certain things that were happening in her life. One day when she came home from school, she told her mother about a film she had seen in health class. The film was confusing, and Taylor had a few questions about it. Her mother's response was that she didn't need to know about the "birds and bees" yet and that she would learn soon enough.

A few weeks later, Taylor found a book on her bed that her mother had checked out of the library. The book was fifteen years old, and it basically made Taylor feel that becoming a woman was something to be ashamed of. The boys at school, snapping her new training bra through her blouse, did not help her growing perceptions of self–hatred. Indeed, Taylor was quickly learning to despise her chubby body. She stopped asking her mother for help, and her father was frequently gone, so she did nothing. At this point, Taylor became consciously aware that she was truly inferior to others.

Taylor believed that the only way she could survive would be to imitate the peers who were regarded as cool. From that point on, her feelings and beliefs were dictated by the feelings and beliefs of others she envied. There was no consistency to her views or any understanding about them. Without any sense of purpose, Taylor learned to imitate the lives of others.

Before long, her own poor self–concept, fueled by her parents' criticisms, caused her to withdraw emotionally into a world of isolation. She did not cry or show her true feelings about anything. Taylor had learned that any value she could have was tied to the acceptance of others around her. Maintaining their favor was taking away her own true identity.

Taylor at Age 14

"My friends are going out tomorrow night, but I know my parents won't let me go. They are going to get some beer and cigarettes and go to the drive–in. Mom says I have to stay home and study. That's all I'm good for. I've got to find a way out of this. I know I'm never going to fit in if I can't be with my friends. Everybody thinks they are cool. I want to be liked, too! Last time, I drank too much and did some bad things. I know I'm not supposed to, but hey, my parents both drink and smoke. How can they get so mad at me? They are hypocrites, and I can't stand them. They are just rubber people, who give nothing and take, take, take..."

Although Taylor had spent her entire childhood trying to please her parents and gain their acceptance and approval, she was reaching the point of doubting it was possible. So, rather than give in to their demands on her, she rebelled and shifted her efforts to pleasing her friends. The crowd she was traveling in was more than willing to value Taylor, since they, too, knew what it felt like to be rejected by their parents.

Taylor at Age 16

"I know that I'm doing things that are not right, but I can't seem to stop myself. And I like the way my friends make me feel. Sometimes they are mean and call me names, but some of them think I'm cool. They say I'm a leader and

stuff, because I'm good at finding beer and smokes. Sheesh, it's pretty easy. My parents have so much booze laying around, they never know when any of it is missing. I used to care about what I did. I wanted my parents to be proud of me, but what's the point? Everything I do, they ignore. For a while, I tried to do a lot of things at school. I even got my grades up, but they just talk about my sister's achievements! Then I tried to get in honor clubs, but they didn't care about that, either. No matter what I did to get their attention, they "upped the ante." Well, for the most part, my friends are worse than me, so I don't have to strive anymore. Trouble is, I keep trying to get approval, and I don't know why. I have to get everything just perfect or I get depressed. Actually, I'm depressed most of the time, whether someone likes me or not. I feel like I'm not going anywhere, fast!"

Taylor had bounced back and forth between rejecting her parents entirely to attempting to do things she thought they might value. Neither ever worked, and regardless of her efforts, she received no emotional acceptance. Both her parents had expressed to Taylor the belief that she would never amount to much and that she should get the fat off and look for a husband to take care of her.

At the age of thirty, still chubby and still wondering who she was, Taylor had been around. She had attempted to find herself in immoral relationships, in drugs, in college, and in God, but deep inside, she still felt isolated and rejected. At one point, in an effort to end it all, she consumed an entire bottle of bourbon. Even over death, she had no control; all that happened was that she became very ill.

What were the core beliefs Taylor had developed about herself, about her family, and ultimately about God? Keep in mind as we go through a biblical standard that Taylor grew up learning very little about the Lord. Apart from attending Sunday school as a small child and being dumped off at church once a week, Taylor did not understand who God was or, more importantly, who she was to Him. Her perception of fathers was that they are harsh, critical, and partial to one kid over another and that you can never please them. Likewise, Taylor's image of mothers was that they are cold, distant, critical, and indifferent to your needs. They drink too much, but tell you not to drink. They demand more of you than you can do, and they expect you to take care of them. They are always sick and complain about their husband. Taylor's perception of God was based on her experiences with her parents.

Let's take a look at the core beliefs Taylor had developed about attachment and bonding, belonging and significance, love and acceptance, and self–concept and identity.

Little Taylor's Core Beliefs About Emotional Nurturing Needs

"I don't know what attach means. I don't remember being attached to anybody. I've always been alone. My daddy attaches to me when he spanks, and Mommy when she bathes me, but I don't know hugs, or soft touches, or warm smiles.

"I am not very important in my family. My sister is special. She is what my parents want, not me. They don't like me very much. I think if they could get rid of me for another kid like my sister, they would do it. I think I might have been a mistake. My mommy and daddy don't seem to enjoy having me around. They always look for things I should change. I don't know how to, and I don't know what to change. Nothing is ever enough.

"Love is getting food, I guess, and a house and clothes. My mommy tells me I should be grateful because Daddy has to work so hard to take care of me. It's sad. I wish he would be home more and be by me, but when he is, it's not like I imagine. Maybe someday he will come home and lift me in his arms and

hug me. Maybe one day, he will say,"Taylor, you can get my white uniform as dirty as you want, because I love you!" I dream that he will say it and play with me, but he don't.

"I don't know who I am...nothing much good, I guess. I just do what I'm told. I just smile and try to be nice and polite. I try to make Mommy happy and Daddy proud. I try to be better and better, but it never matters much. When I grow up, I think I will marry and have kids. Daddy says I have to not be fat, or nobody will want me. I try to not eat. Mommy puts all this food in front of me and says, "Eat every bite." I don't eat except what they give me. It's confusing. Why am I fat? Did God want me to be unhappy? Will it make me not care about things? I wish I had things like my sister, but I guess God made a mistake with me. Nothing works right."

Adult Taylor's Perceptions
Of Her Emotional Nrturing Needs In Childhood

Taylor's adult views of herself were quite different at first. This is how she saw her upbringing:

"Well, when I was a child, the war was going on, and my dad was an important officer. He has a lot of medals for things he did at sea. I am sure it was expected that he would have this perfect little wife, with perfect little children, and perfect little lives... I was a constant frustration to them. But I did the best I could. Learning to please my parents was the way I was raised. There's nothing wrong with that. I have a lot of respect for authority, mostly... and I can see through my parents' problems. They had it pretty difficult when they were children. My dad got beat all the time by his mother, and his dad died when he was real young. His mother had a tough go of it and did the best she could, but life was hard. There wasn't time for showing her feelings. My mom had a hard life, too. I suspect that her daddy abused her, but she won't say. She's

kind of in a twilight world all the time. When she drinks, she can relax, a little. That must be why she does it.

"I learned that love is caring for someone. My parents cared for me the best they could. It's my responsibility to make something of myself now. I can't blame them for not giving me what they didn't get. What I can't figure is why I feel so lousy inside all the time. I do okay, but I always have this looming fear that it's all going to end one day. Something's going to happen, and I'll be alone without a job. It's that old message my dad told me. He said I'd never amount to much. I feel like I'm waiting for something bad to happen. I've already done more than either of them thought. I've even accomplished more than my sister, and they still like her best. I don't know what my problem is, but it doesn't make sense. I'm depressed all the time. I keep trying to be perfect, and I can't reach it. I up the ante every time I succeed at something. I don't even have a life anymore, because I work all the time. It's a good thing I don't have a family. They'd never put up with my schedule. I guess that's one thing my dad was right about. I'm still fat, and nobody wanted me..."

Do you notice the conclusions Taylor developed as she became older? Little by little, she stopped trying to understand why she was so miserable and more or less accepted that there was something inherently lacking in her. The self-fulfilling prophecy for Taylor had come true. She deeply believed that she was ugly and fat, suitable for work—lots of it—but not for intimacy or meaningful relationship. Nearing middle age, she still felt unworthy of being loved by God or anyone else but could not understand why she was depressed.

Let's look next at God's perception of the need for emotional-nurturing and see what Taylor had to learn in order to heal.

Biblical Standard For Emotional Nurturing Needs

Children learn about themselves, life, God, and others largely through their parents. Scripture is full of exhortations for parents to walk in the ways of God so their children will be blessed. Likewise, the Lord's personal involvement and emotional intimacy with His children has always been regarded as the foundation from which adults should draw their parenting skills.

Ultimately, to create core beliefs that will impact a child most positively, several things need to happen. First and foremost, from the earliest days of their life, babies need to experience love and attachment. Parents cannot and will not give what they do not understand. They most likely will not offer what they have not experienced.

Let's now turn to Scripture and examine what love really means, as David wrote in Psalm 36:5–10:

Lord, your love reaches to the heavens.

Your loyalty goes to the skies.

Your goodness is as high as the mountains.

Your justice is as deep as the great ocean.

Lord, you protect both men and animals.

God, your love is so precious!

You protect people as a bird

protects her young under her wings.

They eat the rich food in your house.

You let them drink from your river of pleasure.

You are the giver of life.

Your light lets us enjoy life.

Continue to love those who know you.

And continue to do good to those who are good.

David was able to clearly grasp the love of God and was motivated by that love to give of himself to others. His emotional devotion to his children was highly regarded, even if he failed to discipline them at times. Indirectly, the book of Proverbs was largely the fruit of David's love for his son Solomon. In the earliest years of his life, King Solomon demonstrated an unusual wisdom that came as the result of both his own loving experiences with his parents and a keen sense of God as His heavenly Father.

Let's look at two different kinds of love that Scripture addresses:

1. Agape Love—God's love for us
2. Human love—A biblical mandate for us

It's important to remember as we look at God's word that His standard was never intended to be burdensome. We were designed with the natural capacity to love and receive love. Indeed, as some describe it, we have natural "love tanks" that are empty when we come into the world and in need of filling. Primarily through abuse and neglect, we have lost sensitivity to this innate security need. If we recognize that our lives and relationships are void of the kind of love the Bible speaks of, the answer is to take the necessary trek down memory lane to look for the holes in our "love tanks." The inability to love is learned for the most part and is not at all an inherent characteristic.

God's Love

The richest, purest form of love is found in God's love. There is no flaw in His devotion to us or in His actions toward us. What are the characteristics of this perfect love?

God's love is unfailing and endures. It abounds and is ever before us. It is wonderful and priceless, directed and great. It is better than life, is faithful, and stands firm. It supports us in our pain and is just when recalling our mistakes. It is compassionate, protective, everlasting, and quieting. God's love is for those who love and fear Him, and it fills the earth. We are told that His love slows His hand in judgment. It is poured out on us and is demonstrative. His love cannot be robbed from us or driven away. His love compels us, it completes us, it is sacrificial and without remorse; it is perfect and has the power to drive out fear. It initiates when we cannot and chooses our best in righteous indignation. His love disciplines us at times, but always for our good, and seeks to comfort us with the assurance of His forgiveness. His love is patient and kind, trustworthy, and deserving of our hope. God's love is the greatest of all qualities and characteristics. And God loves perfectly! (Exodus 15:13; Psalms 6:4; 13:5; I Ch.16:34; Neh.9:17; Psalms 31:21; 36:7; 42:8; 89:2; 101:1; Zeph.3:17; Psalm 119:64; Romans 5:5,8; I John 2:5; 4:9; Psalm 33:5; Proverbs 3:12; I John 4:18–19; II Corinthians 5:14)

Taylor did not believe in a God with these qualities. If anything, her perception was that He was rigid, cold, distant, and mean. She was sure that any mistakes on her part would result in His wrath. Her minimal church experience had taught her about baby Jesus, but she had stopped going to church before she learned about her glorious Savior.

Taylor's core belief about love was that it was nonexistent. It was for those more beautiful, gifted, slender, intelligent, and fortunate. She was sure that her parents' lack of love was tied to her unloveliness, not to their problems. She didn't know anything about her parents, really. Neither of them shared their feelings. There had been plenty of complaining, but it was usually directed at her. Taylor did not believe in love and had concluded deep in her heart that there was no God of love. The verses she and I went through together only made her more angry. Taylor felt that God had somehow failed to give her decent parents. Because she had never felt loved or experienced love from her parents—even as a small child—her only concept of it was what she had learned in romance novels and on television. What she had learned was something she would never be allowed to experience.

Human Love

As Christians, we are to mirror the qualities of love that God demonstrates, although, of course, we cannot do it perfectly. The characteristics we are to exemplify can be seen in I Corinthians 13. We are told that love is not noisy, self–seeking, or selfish, not proud or arrogant, not possessive or envious. It is not boastful or rude and is not easily angered. Love does not keep a record of wrongs, and it is patient, kind, protective, and continuous. Love hates evil and rejoices in the truth. Of all the attributes we should seek to emulate, the ability to love is regarded as the highest.

Paul's letter to the Philippians addresses the attitude that Christians should carry toward one another:

> *This is my prayer for you:*
> *that your love will grow more and more;*
> *that you will have knowledge*
> *and understanding with your love;*
> *that you will see the difference between*
> *good and bad and choose the good;*
> *that you will be pure and without wrong*
> *for the coming of Christ;*
> *that you will do many good things*
> *with the help of Christ*
> *to bring glory and praise to God.*

Philippians 1:9–11

The kind of love the apostle Paul speaks of in this passage is active and ultimately is lived out for the glory of God. Later in the same letter, Paul continues his thoughts on love:

> *Does your life in Christ give you strength?*
> *Does his love comfort you?*
> *Do we share together in the Spirit?*
> *Do you have mercy and kindness?*
> *If so, make me very happy*
> *by having the same thoughts,*
> *sharing the same love,*
> *and having one mind and purpose.*
> *When you do things,*

> *do not let selfishness or pride be your guide.*
> *Be humble and give more honor*
> *to others than to yourselves.*
> *Do not be interested only in your own life,*
> *but be interested in the lives of others.*
> *In your lives you must think*
> *and act like Christ Jesus.*
> *Christ himself was like God in everything.*
> *He was equal with God.*
> *But he did not think that being equal with God*
> *was something to be held on to.*
> *He gave up his place with God*
> *and made himself nothing.*
> *He was born to be a man*
> *and became like a servant.*
> *And when he was living as a man,*
> *he humbled himself*
> *and was fully obedient to God.*
> *He obeyed even when that caused his death—*
> *death on a cross.*
> Philippians 2:1–8

❦   ❦   ❦   ❦   ❦

*Love is not a casual thing. It is a willful choice
to go against the ways of the world and the
ways of our sinful nature.*

❦   ❦   ❦   ❦   ❦

From the time Taylor was a small child and was sent to Sunday school, she had been taught the "golden rule," namely, that she was to love others as she loved herself. This was difficult because Taylor did not love herself and had no clue how to love others. She had learned that it was her responsibility to obey Scripture, but her own lack of nurturing as a child kept her from opening up to others. In fact, she had endeavored to obey every rule—just as her daddy had taught—but her experience with Christianity had been the same as with her parents. Taylor doubted that God could love or care for her. When she read in the Scriptures about Jesus dying for her sins and about God the Father nurturing her as a babe nursing on her mother's breast, Taylor was appalled at the thought. The only image that came to her mind when she thought of her mother was of her nursing a bottle of beer.

Love is not a casual thing. It is a willful choice to go against the ways of the world and the ways of our sinful nature. It chooses the highest good of those it encounters and finds peace as its reward. Paul tells the believers at Colosse that they have a new life in Christ and are being made new in the image of the One who made them. His encouragement includes the following exhortation:

> *God has chosen you*
> *and made you his holy people.*
> *He loves you.*
> *So always do these things:*
> *Show mercy to others; be kind,*
> *humble, gentle, and patient.*
> *Do not be angry with each other*
> *because the Lord forgave you.*
> *Do all these things;*
> *but most important, love each other.*
> *Love is what holds you all*
> *together in perfect unity.*
> *Let the peace that Christ gives*
> *control your thinking.*
> Colossians 2:12–15

Taylor's core belief about compassion, kindness, gentleness, and patience was that they didn't exist because she had never experienced them. Although the words were known to her theoretically, the feelings behind the words were not there.

Taylor had decided never to have children because of a core belief that parents make children miserable and, therefore, children can never be happy. Because of her own loneliness and despair, Taylor did not want to inflict the same on her children. The idea that she didn't have to treat her own little ones the same way as her dysfunctional parents had treated her was a new concept to Taylor.

Peter's letters seem to be, in part, a reflection of his own struggles earlier in his life. His exhortation was that we purify ourselves by obeying the truth so that we would have sincere love for one another, that we would love one another deeply with all our heart (I Peter 1:22). In his second letter, Peter gave the following instructions:

> *Jesus has the power of God. His power has given us*
> *everything we need to live and to serve God. We have*
> *these things because we know him. Jesus called us by his*
> *glory and goodness.... Because you have these blessings,*
> *you should try as much as you can to add these things to*
> *your lives: to your faith, add goodness; and to your good-*
> *ness, add knowledge; and to your knowledge, add self–*
> *control; and to your self–control, add the ability to hold*
> *on; and to your ability to hold on, add service for God;*
> *and to your service for God, add kindness for your broth-*
> *ers and sisters in Christ; and to this kindness, add love. If*
> *all these things are in you and are growing, they will help*
> *you never to be useless.*
>
> II Peter 1:3–7

Core beliefs are hard to change. As Taylor and I went through this passage, pausing at each character quality, Taylor tried to imagine either of her parents as having any of them. Knowledge was very important, but it wasn't about the Lord. Taylor had "learned" how to avoid her parents' wrath by manipulating them. Self–control was like discipline, or so she thought. In her mind, self–control meant you stopped yourself just before hitting someone or you stopped drinking after three bottles of beer. Perseverance is what she did when her mother lectured her for hours. There was no kindness, no goodness, no love.

In the same way, John, who had the privilege of being "the disciple whom Jesus loved," wrote that we should love not the world or the things of the world but rather the things of God. He reminded us of the greatness of God's love that had been lavished on us. Being called children of God was, to John, an incredible revelation. God's message was the one that had been entrusted to John:

> *This is the teaching you have heard from the beginning:*
> *We must love each other.... My children,*
> *our love should not be only words and talk.*
> *Our love must be true love.*
> *And we should show that love by what we do....*
> *Dear friends, we should love each other,*
> *because love comes from God.*
> *The person who loves has become God's child*
> *and knows God.*
> *Whoever does not love does not know God,*
> *because God is love.*
> *This is how God showed his love to us:*
> *He sent his only Son into the world*
> *to give us life through him.*
> *True love is God's love for us, not our love for God.*
> *God sent his Son to be the way to take away our sins.*
> *That is how much God loved us, dear friends!*
> *So we also must love each other.*
> *No one has ever seen God.*
> *But if we love each other, God lives in us.*
> *If we love each other, God's love has reached its goal.*
> *It is made perfect in us....*
> *And so we know the love that God has for us,*
> *and we trust that love. God is love.*
> *Whoever lives in love lives in God,*

and God lives in him....
And God gave us this command:
Whoever loves God must also love his brother....
Loving God means obeying his commands.
And God's commands are not too hard for us.
Everyone who is a child of God
has the power to win against the world.
It is our faith that wins
the victory against the world.
I John, various texts

Core beliefs can lead to interesting conclusions. By the time Taylor had looked at I John, she was convinced that she must not be a Christian. She was sure that she did not love others and confessed that she was not sure what love really was. She had no loving memories to recall, or so few of them that the other images overpowered the good memories. Taylor began to realize that she harbored a relentless immaturity. She was still looking for a mommy to love her and a daddy to give value to her existence. Over several months, as her anger was vented, a tenderness began to show little by little. For Taylor, being able to tell the Lord that she could not feel His love and to cry openly before Him was the beginning of restoration.

❧   ❧   ❧   ❧   ❧

Love always reveals itself, and when
it is present, it reflects God. It promotes
and acts in a way that clearly
desires the highest good.

❧   ❧   ❧   ❧   ❧

Love always reveals itself, and when it is present, it reflects God. It promotes and acts in a way that clearly desires the highest good. Even when the outcome is less than desired, the motive can be seen in its true light, and the conclusion accepted that it was an act of love.

Unlike God, we do not have the ability to love perfectly,

and we are dependent on Him to teach us how to love. Living in a world where people seldom choose anyone's good, it is difficult and oftentimes a lonely endeavor. Still, we can be comforted in knowing that our thoughts, motives, and actions are known to the One who sees all things, and it is to Him that we ultimately have to give account.

For Taylor, the journey home was a painful one. There was a lot for her to resolve with her parents, but the process had begun. As she opened the door to her heart, the floodgates of God's love poured over her. For several months, she immersed herself in His love and acceptance.

Then the grieving began. She experienced honest anger toward her parents for all she had failed to receive, and self–contempt for not seeing the truth earlier in her life. One of the most difficult parts of Taylor's recovery was her parents' inability to deal with the pain they had inflicted on her. Even when Taylor attempted to confront their actions lovingly, their responses were hostile and defensive. Although it grieved Taylor that her parents were not willing to be reconciled to her even though she offered forgiveness, release still came as she offered her broken heart to the Lord.

Taylor learned that she had the ability to change problem areas in her life regardless of the reaction of others. She no longer had to suffer for the damage that had been inflicted by her parents. She no longer had to live her life as a victim. She was now a survivor!

In any recovery process, the wounded person progresses through various stages of grieving: looking at the problem, understanding why it is there, and dealing with denial, anger, pain, sadness, and loss. Before Taylor was able to truly forgive her parents, she recycled through the stages several times, each step carrying her nearer to healing and freedom. The groundwork was being laid for a new life, with a foundation of truth, walls made of hope and faith, and a protective covering of love that even Taylor could approve of.

Common Problems Of Unmet Emotional Nurturing Needs

Adults who did not have their emotional–nurturing needs met in childhood often display the following symptoms. If you are able to relate to any of the symptoms listed, check the corresponding box.

Poor self–concept (either external
or internal locus of control) . . . . ❑
Rejection and feelings of abandonment . . . . . . ❑
Feelings of worthlessness . . . . ❑
Withdrawal and isolation . . . . ❑
Inappropriate venting of anger . . . . ❑
Promiscuous sexual relationships . . . . ❑
Distrust of authority figures . . . . ❑
Problems attaching in healthy relationships . . . ❑
Depression . . . . ❑
Perfectionist tendencies . . . . ❑
Negative and critical toward self and others . . . ❑
Extreme distortions about God,
self, and others . . . . ❑
Lack of purpose and goals . . . . ❑
Compulsive behavior . . . . ❑

Part Three

Completing The Journey

We know that our body—
the tent we live in here on earth—
will be destroyed.
But when that happens,
God will have a house for us to live in.
It will not be a house made by men.
It will be a home in heaven that will last forever.
But now we are tired of this body.
We want God to give us our heavenly home.
It will clothe us, and we will not be naked.
While we live in this body, we have burdens,
and we complain. We do not want to be naked.
We want to be clothed with our heavenly home.
Then this body that dies will be fully covered with life.
This is what God made us for.
II Corinthians 5:1–5

Chapter 11

Teaching Yourself The Truth

Rewriting Your Story

So Jesus said to the Jews who believed in him,
"If you continue to obey my teaching,
you are truly my followers.
Then you will know the truth.
And the truth will make you free."
John 8:31-32

*I*n journeying down the road to restoration, one must first consider the cost of the venture and determine whether one has the means to accomplish the desired end result. Several ingredients are necessary to complete the trip. The journey begins with certain preparations—those ongoing steps that should be a regular part of every Christian's life. Among these steps are daily devotions and Scripture reading, which may already be a way of your life. You find, however, that you still have problems. Since you are already taking these steps, you part feel discouraged from going any further. Many Christians who read the Bible have a great deal of head knowledge about the Bible and the rules they are supposed to live by, but if they never apply what they have learned to their daily living, they will experience minimal change.

Many of us have problems with our emotions. We *know* the truth, but can't feel it, and consequently we cannot get ourselves to embrace it. Being a "good girl" or "good boy" is not the ultimate goal. By learning to take down the walls around our heart little by little, we can, and probably will, experience a level of emotional intimacy with the Lord and others that we have never before known.

Don't look for a special "experience"
as you journey down the road,
and try not to gauge your success
by a particular feeling.

As an adult child of abuse or neglect, you may never have experienced such feelings and thus don't know what to compare them with. As with any love relationship, it's impossible to say with absolute certainty what feelings will be present. Consequently, your emotional attachment to the Lord will no doubt feel different from someone else's. Your gender, personality, temperament, and life experience all play a part in determining what your feelings will be like.

Set your goals modestly. Tell the Lord your concerns and feelings as honestly as you can. Don't be afraid to ask Him for the ability to feel Him in your heart or to understand His will for you. If in a private moment with the Lord you begin to weep, let yourself grieve openly before Him. It may feel uncomfortable or awkward at first, but it needs to happen. If it is anger rather than sadness that rules your heart, risk telling Him how you feel.

Although it can be dangerous to base theology on your personal experiences, you can learn valuable lessons from the Lord in His personal dealings with you. If hardness and indifference distance you from Him, you may find that you have a greater tendency toward pride and independence. Allowing yourself to come to the Lord with an open heart produces a spontaneous desire to repent without so much as a word from Him.

Don't look for a special "experience" as you journey down the road, and try not to gauge your success by a particular feeling. When your heart is open and ready to embrace God, it will be clear to you—and probably to most of those who know you well. Also, if emotional intimacy is an area of your life that has been difficult for a long time, it may take a while to work through your core belief distortions.

Plan to settle in for the long haul and spare yourself unnecessary expectations about getting through this process quickly. Depending on the areas of wounding and severity, you may experience rapid growth, or your growth may take a long time. Realistically, the process will continue throughout your life. New revelations of areas the Lord wants to heal or restore will appear until He takes you home.

Sometimes people who are working through problems become so focused on their pain and woundedness that they withdraw from ministry and reaching out to others. Your opportunity to heal is no reason to stop serving the Lord or giving of yourself. Even if you feel that your resources are limited or nonexistent, consider this a challenge to deepen your dependency on God.

Sometimes the problem is the opposite. "Doing" has largely functioned as a replacement for "being." This is a common reason workaholics have difficulty addressing their form of addictive behavior. Slowing down long enough to evaluate core belief distortions produces such discomfort and anxiety that such people are quick to return to the grind before the lessons have been learned or changes can be made.

In either case, your attitude should always reflect a servant's heart that welcomes opportunities to wisely give to others regardless of life's struggles. It is in the act of giving to others that the Lord is able to lift us out of the mire of introspection in which we may find ourselves.

The following steps are suggested as a way to help organize the healing process. Remember that this is not a race for you to hurry through. Take each step slowly and return to it as often as needed. Learning to live a truly healthy life requires conscious and regular care and attention.

1. **Salvation through Jesus Christ and make a commitment to obedience.**

A basic faith in Jesus Christ as Lord and Savior is necessary to undo not only the emotional damage but also the spiritual violations. Herein lies the secret to all healing. At times the wounding of our souls is so intense that any hope for healing requires an unrelenting belief in God's love for us and His willingness to help us in our time of need. In other words, we are dependent on Him to restore what has been broken (Hebrews 4:14-16; Psalm 23:3). True restoration always takes place in the context of relationship. As adult victims, we struggle with the belief that salvation is enough or that the Lord cares. Remember that these are distortions we learned because of abuse or neglect, not because they are true.

2. **Accept with an unyielding belief that the Bible is God's authoritative word to us, flawless and good for**

correction and instruction, regardless of culture or generation.

We must accept God's commandments as absolutes and His principles as guiding lights in our journey of life. If our beliefs contradict Scripture, we must commit to changing our values to properly reflect biblical norms (II Samuel 22:31; Psalm 119:9, 105; Ephesians 6:17; John 17:17; II Timothy 3:14-17). This principle may be difficult because you may have maintained a mental belief that the Bible is accurate. Remember that your resistance and difficulty are based on what you have learned. In our healing process, we want to develop a tremendous love and excitement over the instructions and promises we receive through God's word!

❧ ❧ ❧ ❧ ❧

Developing the strength and courage
to grow empowers us to mature
and act responsibly.

❧ ❧ ❧ ❧ ❧

3. **Respond to truth the Holy Spirit reveals about your sins and the damage you have caused.**

Be willing to write down the specifics if the Lord reveals areas of your life that are inflicting pain or preventing you from healing. Dealing with self-protection and core belief distortions is difficult, but the Lord promises to help us as we call out to Him. The purpose of this step is to ensure that our hearts are right with God and that nothing is hindering our prayers for help (Psalm 66:18-20; II Chronicles 7:14; Psalm 32:5; Proverbs 14:9; Romans 6:11-23; Hebrews 12:1; James 1:12-15).

Even though the effects of the abuse have endured since childhood, the actual abuse ended long ago. Nevertheless, many of us have erected walls to protect ourselves at all costs, and in so doing, we may have hurt others. By keeping our emotions closed off from others, we selfishly refuse to give of ourselves in healthy ways. We may harbor anger and bitterness that damage our current relationships, and we may tend to hang on to past wounds much longer than is necessary. By allowing the Lord to show us the things that keep us victims, we are able to begin the process of changing from the inside. Developing the strength and courage to grow empowers us to mature and act responsibly. The wonderful consequence is that we actually will "feel better" as a result. Having the ability to "do the right thing" from the heart (and experiencing the internal strength that produces) allows the immature aspects of our emotions an outlet to challenge and conquer core belief distortions.

4. Make amends as God directs in prayer and through His word.

Unfortunately, many Christians believe it is enough to ask God to forgive their sins. Their unwillingness to make amends with those they have offended is often an indication of a lack of repentance. True remorse always longs to see the wounded person restored and the wrongs righted (Proverbs 14:9; Numbers 5:5-7; Exodus 22:3; Leviticus 6:5).

Many victims say that all they really want is for the perpetrator to be sorry for what he/she did. Acknowledging the offense validates our pain and vindicates our belief that wrongs have been done to us. By asking for forgiveness, you are restoring your relationship with God. Heaven rejoices, and God is given the glory.

The same standard must apply to us. As we grapple with the difficulties of turning from self-protection to obeying Scripture, we must go to those we have wounded and earnestly seek their forgiveness. This must be done in humility, with no excuses pleaded, and with sincerity. The process of getting right with the Lord produces a softness and a compassion that allows us to empathize with those who struggle to confess. Ultimately, allowing God to tenderize our hearts and minds prepares the way for reconciliation with those who have abused us.

Bitterness is a constant barrier to healing, as is the unwillingness to turn from our own sins. Victims tend to focus on self-perceived misery as a way to avoid further pain.

Humility is painful to our human pride. This is why Jesus embraced the little children and said we must become like them to enter the kingdom of heaven (Matthew 18:1-4). Trusting and unpretentious, the children innocently responded to His every word.

5. Establish a daily pattern of time with the Lord.

Disciplining yourself to a regular time daily with the Lord is an important part of the Christian life as well as the healing process. Regardless of the time of day you choose, your daily devotions should include a meaningful Bible study, prayer for others and for your own petitions, worship, and meditation on Scripture. It's also helpful to memorize particular passages the Lord shows you. Sometimes you may feel that the last thing in the world you want to do is to pray or read Scripture, but as with other important commitments, it's essential to maintain this discipline. God will honor your willingness to stick with Him when you least feel like it!

Keep in mind the fact that God's word is what brings healing and restoration. Satan would love nothing more than for us to avoid studying Scripture, as is the customary practice of many believers! In truth, we need to immerse ourselves with a commitment to study, embrace, and obey the life-giving principles of the Bible.

We also need to be wise about the kind of information we take in apart from the word of God. Many people in recovery say they want to change but continually immerse themselves in secular resources that intensify their internal struggle. People who seem to respond best to God's healing solutions are those who are cautious about the kinds of books they read, movies and television they watch, and music they listen to.

6. Keep a private journal as you go through this process.

Keeping a journal allows you to see growth and to track your progress which will be immensely helpful. Many have also found that seeing on paper how they really feel is somewhat revealing. Include Scriptures that have become meaningful, struggles you have worked through, prayers to—and emotions toward—the Lord throughout the process, and answers to your heavenly petitions. Write about core feelings and beliefs you carry in each category we cover in addition to others that are raised throughout your healing journey.

If you recognized problems in any of the categories we discussed in this book, write them down in your journal. (For instance, if you have a problem trusting, identified on the "Safety and Protection inventory," make a journal note along with possible reasons you may have developed this problem.) Start with your family of origin patterns and move forward. Ask such questions as, Was my environment safe and nurturing? Was I afraid of my parents or other adult relatives or my siblings as a small child? Was there emotional abuse going on in my home in the form of fighting, yelling, name–calling, or unrealistic expectations placed on me? Was I or were any of my siblings sexually or physically abused by anyone?

7. **After identifying the symptoms, begin to ask the Lord to show you the root(s) of each inappropriate behavior.**

Take one symptom at a time, since it's easy to become overwhelmed if you try to do too much too fast. If, for example, you recognize that you have trouble trusting or being vulnerable with people (which is the symptom) and can point to some form of abuse as a child (which is the root), you should be able to sort out the core belief you are operating with. Here's the formula:

SYMPTOM	+	ROOT	=	CORE BELIEF
Inappropriate Behavior		Form of abuse or neglect		What you really believe

You can use this formula for each symptom you are struggling with. If you are not sure which behavior is the problem but recognize that there was abuse in your background, you can reverse the formula:

ROOT +	**CORE BELIEF** =	**SYMPTOM**
Form of abuse or neglect	What you really believe	Inappropriate Behavior

Ultimately, to truly change, it's important that you identify the core beliefs you learned between birth and age ten and determine how those beliefs are manifested in your adult life.

8. **Once it is reasonably clear what the problem is and how you learned it, take each area and do a word study in Scripture on that topic.**

Take the problem or attitude you struggle with, write it down, and meditate on the relevant Bible passages that identify the following:

a. The definition of the problem.

b. How the problem is learned or experienced.

c. With whom or how we are supposed to trust our problem on a human level.

d. Whether children ultimately learn through God or through their parents that they have a problem.

e. How we can learn to trust God for help with the problem.

Ask yourself as many questions as you can about each area and try to look earnestly for the answers in Scripture.

9. **Compare your present core beliefs with Scripture.**

What are the areas of inconsistency? Ask the Lord to show you those feelings or behaviors that are damaging or that conflict with Scripture and write them down. For instance:

a. I am supposed to trust in the Lord with all my heart, but I don't do that. I can't trust Him, because He has let me down in the past.

> b. Scripture says my parents were supposed to protect me and provide my needs, but I blame God for their failure to do so. I believe that He should have met my needs anyway.

Do this exercise in one area at a time. There is no value in hurrying, so go slowly. Start with the deepest core belief distortions, such as trust, safety, belonging, acceptance, and love. Once you have resolved the bottom–line distortions, the other areas will change more quickly.

10. **Commit to changing your core beliefs and practices to reflect a Biblical view.**

What specifically do you need to do to change? Write it down. If it is unclear to you what is correct, talk with a pastor or trusted friend who is committed to the integrity of Scripture. For instance:

> I have a core belief that I cannot trust God; therefore, I continue to make major decisions about my employment without asking God about it. Instead, to find out where I should work, I need to seek God diligently to find His will for me, because I am learning that He made me and He knows what is best for me.

11. **Decide whether or not you are willing to truly change in the areas you listed.**

If you are willing, ask God to forgive you for the specific sins He showed you. He does not play mind or heart games with us. If we are willing to be convicted of sin, the Holy Spirit will faithfully reveal it. General feelings of condemnation or hopelessness usually come from ourselves or from Satan. True repentance involves a desire to change, remorse for how your sins have grieved the Lord and wounded others, a thankfulness that God has forgiven you, and anticipation that you will feel better as you obey His direction.

If you are not willing to change, list your reasons and be honest about them with God. Sometimes the problem is that we don't think we can change because of repeated failure in trying to overcome specific sins. Feeling hopeless and guilty, you may try to avoid dealing with the problem rather than face feelings of defeat or bondage.

Many victims of childhood abuse have learned that they have no power and consequently give up very easy. Control was taken from them, and they feel incapable of changing their situation, just as in childhood. (This is a core belief!) No one likes to feel that way, but it's normal.

If you are willing to be willing but recognize that you can't do it alone, welcome to the human race! We all have such issues in our life. There are several things you can do:

a. Talk with a trusted friend or spiritual adviser about your dilemma and ask the person to help you.

b. If your problem is severe, you may want to seek a professional Christian counselor who uses Scripture in therapy.

c. Look for a Christian support group to participate in until you have worked through your problems.

d. Seek out friends who will faithfully pray for you about your problems. If you are struggling with the desire to change, have your friends ask specifically that God would change your heart.

Remember that our battle is spiritual and the enemy does not want us to love and serve God. The fight will not be won easily! Left to ourselves, we probably would not be victorious, but by accessing the power of the Holy Spirit we can continue to be renewed, transformed, and energized by the authority of God and through His help! It is the Lord who heals us and enables us to be free from the wounds of our past.

If you are not convinced that you have to alter your behavior but know that your current practices are biblically questionable, put the particular issue aside for a while and go on to another area. (Remember, you can always come back to it.) Ask the Lord to help you to have a clear understanding of His will in that area. It may not be the same for everyone, so seek

Him persistently for personal direction! God does not contradict His Word, so remember to keep Scripture as the standard against which you compare your behavior. Embrace all absolutes and ask Him to show you how related principles apply to your life.

   12. **Summarize the following:**

   a. The symptoms.

   b. The roots.

   c. Your core beliefs.

   d. God's standard as revealed in the Bible.

   e. Comparison of your core beliefs with Scripture.

   f. Your actual behaviors or attitudes that need to be changed.

   13. **Set realistic goals for each problem area identified.**

   For goals to be realistic, they need to include the following:

   a. **Problem statement.** What is the behavior and/or feelings that need to be changed?

   b. **Short-term and long-term goals.** What are the goals you hope to achieve in the next month...six months...year?

   c. **Steps to accomplish goals.** Break the steps down for each problem given. What must you do first, second, third, etc., to accomplish your goal?

   d. **Accountability.** How will you measure your activity? Whom can you involve in the process to hold you accountable for the goals you have set? Can the person(s) help you determine whether your goals are realistic (ask for feedback)?

   e. **Consider the cost.** Determine what resources you need to accomplish your goals (e.g., money, books, counselors, friends, support group, prayer partners, time available, other stresses in life during healing process).

f. **Just do it!** Whoever said the road to hell is paved with good intentions was probably a procrastinator. Even though it may seem overwhelming, you have to start somewhere. The problems won't go away by themselves. Get going!

g. **Evaluate.** Following up on your goal strategies is very important. Evaluate your plans at the end of one week. Write and talk about the progress and/or difficulties you have faced. Do you need to make any adjustments? Did your plan go smoothly? Were there things you could have done or should do the next week to make the changes less difficult? Do you need to reevaluate some of your goals and/or steps?

h. **Worship and give thanksgiving.** Many of us find that it is the Lord who finally gives us the victory over our addictions and struggles. How can we adequately express gratitude for our Abba Father's faithfulness and help throughout the journey? Make sure that you are offering praise and thanksgiving for God's grace and help.

I. **Seek outside professional help if you need it.** If you experienced severe abuse in childhood, you may very well need professional help to work through the damage. If this is the case, look for a Christian therapist who is known for using Scripture. If you have trouble locating such a therapist in your area, you might find it helpful to contact pastors at local Christian churches in your community who could refer you to a godly counselor.

It takes time to heal and to find purposeful direction. You may find it difficult to work through your core belief distortions. If you have even one godly friend you can turn to for help, that's a start.

God's design for dependency has your best interest at heart and is full of wonderful adventures as you journey toward home!

Epilogue

As you have read *Designed For Dependency*, my hope is that you have been able to find answers to some of your baffling questions and relief for your pain. If you were able to recognize the areas in which you act independently of the Lord and have committed to change, this book has been a success.

If you will take the time to ask God to help you resolve past pain, He will respond. If you will allow Him to direct your healing process, it will go more smoothly. If you will allow others to hold you up in your struggle, you will find that the sadness will dim. If you will allow yourself to enjoy dependency on God, the struggles of life will not overwhelm you.

See you when we get Home!